The Association of Jewish Libraries
Guide to
Yiddish
Short Stories

by Bennett Muraskin

ajl

Ben Yehuda Press
Teaneck, New Jersey

Published by Ben Yehuda Press
430 Kensington Road
Teaneck, NJ 07666

http://www.BenYehudaPress.com

Ben Yehuda Press books may be purchased for educational, business or sales promotional use. For information, please contact:
Special Markets, Ben Yehuda Press,
430 Kensington Road, Teaneck, NJ 07666
markets@BenYehudaPress.com

http://www.JewishLibraries.org

The Association of Jewish Libraries promotes Jewish literacy through enhancement of libraries and library resources and through leadership for the profession and practitioners of Judaica librarianship. AJL membership is open to individuals and libraries, library workers, and library supporters.

ISBN13 978-1-934730-31-7

Library of Congress Cataloging-in-Publication Data

Muraskin, Bennett.
The Association of Jewish Libraries guide to Yiddish short stories / by Bennett Muraskin.
    p. cm.
Includes bibliographical references and index.
ISBN 978-1-934730-31-7 (alk. paper)
1. Yiddish fiction--History and criticism. 2. Yiddish fiction--Translations into English--Bibliography. I. Title.
PJ5124.M87 2011
839'.130109--dc23
                              2011037311

  11 12 13 / 10 9 8 7 6 5 4 3   20111113

Contents

Foreword

Yiddish literature is our *yerushe*, our inheritance. As an international cultural product, Yiddish exists independent of religion or territory. This is a source of strength but also weakness, because this means that the language requires a lot of nurturing to survive. Translation is part of that nurture. Let's do our best to keep *yiddishkayt* alive.

Many people helped with this project. Gella Schweid Fishman suggested that I expand and revise the original *Yiddish Short Story Sampler* first published in 1997 and referred me to Dr. Sheva Zucker, *take a Yidish maven*, who, despite her hectic schedule, suggested additional stories and provided the Yiddish titles and sources for many old and new ones. New York Public Library Jewish librarian Amanda Seigel and YIVO librarian Yeshaya Metal also graciously identified the Yiddish titles and sources for a number of the stories in this guide.

I received more help tracking down Yiddish authors, titles and sources of stories from some very accomplished scholars and translators: Kevin Carnes, Frieda Forman, Harvey Fink, Ken Frieden, Hershl Hartman, Curt Leviant, Tony Michels, Eliezer Niborski, David Roskies, Al Stein, Joseph Sherman and Yechiel Szeintuch. To this list, I add Dan Opatoshu (grandson of Yiddish writer Joseph Opatoshu), Bella Bryks-Klein (daughter of Yiddish writer and Holocaust survivor Rachmil Bryks) and my friend Albert Rosenblatt.

Special thanks go to Troim Katz Handler, Fishl Kutner, Barnett Zumoff, Dr. Sheva Zucker and my wife Ellen Muraskin for reviewing the manuscript and assisting in the final editing.

The author alone is responsible for any errors.

Introduction

This is an attempt to provide a survey of the best Yiddish short stories available in English translation that can be used for studying Yiddish literature, teaching Yiddish classes and in programming for Yiddish clubs. The stories address humanistic themes: Speaking truth to power, ethical commitment, the dangers of religious fanaticism, the plight of the poor, anti-Semitism, the struggle for social justice and a more humane society, moral choices, spirituality, the parent-child relationship, the role of women, marriage and intermarriage, etc. In the same spirit, a separate section is devoted to stories relating to Jewish holidays, for adults and children alike.

Much of modern Yiddish literature is a prime expression of Jewish humanism. Its creators were typically rebels against authority, both Jewish and Gentile, and proponents of universal ideals of freedom of thought, social justice and human dignity. Most Yiddish authors did not write for the educated elite, but for the average Jew. They formed a special bond with their readers, which gave Yiddish literature a popular character. Although rooted in the religious tradition, they were, with few exceptions, secular in their outlook and sympathetic to radical movements of the left. It should, therefore, come as no surprise that secular Jewish leftists have historically taken a leading role in preserving this literature and incorporating into it their concept of Jewish culture (yidishkayt). It can almost be said that Yiddish literature served as their "Bible."

But secular leftist Jews were not the first American Jews to produce translations. That honor belongs to Leo Wiener, a Harvard professor and immigrant from Poland, who was so impressed with Morris Rosenfeld's poetry that he translated selections and published them as *Songs of the Ghetto* (1898). The following year, Wiener's *The History of Yiddish Literature in the Nineteenth Century* appeared, including selections from Yiddish writers and poets.

Most other early translations of Yiddish literature into English in the US were published by the Jewish Publication Society (JPS), the oldest Jewish publisher in the US. A non-profit membership organization founded in 1888 by German Jews, the JPS recognized that without translations, the descendants of East European Jewish immigrants would lose touch with their literary traditions. This perspective was unusual for German Jews who generally considered Yiddish a crude vernacular that should disappear. It also saw Jewish literature as an excellent tool for educating the non-Jewish public about the Jewish experience in Europe and America.

The JPS's earliest translations were of I.L. Peretz's *Stories and Pictures* (1906) and *Yiddish Tales* (1912), both translated by Helena Frank, a non-Jew from Great Britain. The JPS also issued two Sholem Asch novels, *Kiddush Ha-Shem* (1912, translated by Rufus Learsi) and *Sabbatai Zevi* (1930); A.S. Sachs' elegy to Jewish life in Lithuania, *Worlds That Passed* (1928, translated by Harold Berman); and three books by Joseph Opatoshu, including the novels *In Polish Woods* (1938, Isaac Goldberg) and *The Last Revolt* (1952, Moshe Spiegel), as well as the short story collection *A Day in Regensburg* (1968, Joseph Sloan). In 1967, JPS published Chaim Grade's *The Well* (Ruth Wisse); in 1969, *the Anthology of Holocaust Literature*, with many excerpts translated from Yiddish; in 1979, a new edition of Ruth Rubin's *Voices of a People: The Story of Yiddish Folksong* and in 1985, a short story collection, *Gifts*, which includes six I.B. Singer stories. Now in its 123rd year, JPS has established a distinguished record of publishing modern Yiddish literature in translation. This record extends to pre-modern Yiddish literature as well. In 1934, JPS published the two-volume classic *Ma'aseh* (mayse) *Bukh*, edited by Moses Gaster, consisting of Yiddish folktales from the Middle Ages.

It was not long before secular Jews took up the cause. Emanuel Haldeman-Julius (1889-1951), the child of Russian Jewish immigrants, rejected Judaism as a youth and became a free thinking Debsian socialist. He is best known as an editor of the popular socialist journal *Appeal to Reason* from his base in Girard, Kansas, hardly a bastion of *yidishkayt*. To make both literary classics and socialist tracts available to the "masses" in inexpensive paperback editions, he founded *Little Blue Books*. Among the thousands of titles he published were Asch's *God of Vengeance* (1918, Isaac Goldberg), *Yiddish Short Stories* (1923, edited and likely translated by Goldberg) and *Great Yiddish Poetry* (1924).

Before the trauma of World War II, Yiddish-based organizations in North America were ambivalent about translating Yiddish literature into English, fearing that it would discourage younger Jews from maintaining literacy in the original and inevitably lead to assimilation. Scattered translations of poetry and prose appeared in the *Jewish Frontier*, the journal of the Labor Zionist movement, the *Menorah Journal*, a Jewish humanist journal, the *Jewish Spectator*, a newsletter edited by the iconoclastic Trude Weiss-Rosmarin and the *Congress Weekly*, the magazine of the American Jewish Congress.

After the loss of so many Yiddish writers and readers in the Holocaust, occasional Yiddish translations and articles about Yiddish continued to appear in these periodicals and newer Jewish magazines notably *Commentary*, founded as a liberal journal in 1946 and *Midstream,* a Zionist magazine founded in 1955. Many of these writings were about the Holocaust or stories by the popular I.B. Singer. Then a major new player arrived on the scene—pro-Soviet Jewish communists, aka the *"linke* (left) *yidn."*

Yiddish prose and poetry in translation became a regular feature of *Jewish Life*, a magazine established by the Yiddish daily, the *Morgn Freiheit*, in 1946 to accommodate its younger adherents who no longer read Yiddish. Translations by either Henry Goodman or Max Rosenfeld continued to be a staple of its successor, *Jewish Currents* established in 1958. (In more recent years, this role has been fulfilled by Gerald Stillman, also known for translating a number of novels by the *zeyde* or "grandfather" of modern Yiddish literature, Mendele Moykher-Sforim.)

In 1947, the Jewish People's Fraternal Order (JPFO) published a short collection of Peretz stories. The YKUF, the *Yiddisher Kultur Farband* (Yiddish Cultural Alliance), founded in 1937, published an enormous output of Yiddish literature before venturing into English translation in 1961, with the publication of *The New Country*, a large collection of Yiddish short stories about Jewish life in America. This was followed by a 1964 collection of Morris Rosenfeld's poetry and prose, an Isaac Raboy novel, *Nine Brothers* (1968) and a 1974 collection of stories by Chaver Paver (Gershon Einbinder). Once again, the translators were either Henry Goodman or Max Rosenfeld.

The best collection of translated Yiddish short stories for children remains *Yiddish Stories For Young People* (1966) edited by Yiddish scholar Itche Goldberg (translated mostly by Benjamin Efron and Henry Goodman). Goldberg, the editor of *Yidishe Kultur*, a first class Yiddish literary journal until his death in 2006, was long associated with *Jewish Life/Currents*, YKUF, the JPFO and other institutions of the Jewish left.

When Nathan Ausubel, then *a linker yid*, wrote his classic *A Treasury of Jewish Folklore* (1948), much of it from Yiddish sources, he meant it to illustrate the underground anti-elitist tradition he detected within Jewish tradition. This extraordinarily popular book is still in print over 60 years later. Ruth Rubin, another product of the old Jewish left, became the foremost collector of Yiddish folksongs, writing *A Treasury of Yiddish Folksongs* (1950) and *Voices of a People* (1963).

It is sad but true that the *linke Yidn* embraced Soviet communism, despite its anti-Semitic practices, and only began to disavow it in 1956 after Khruschev's earthshaking denunciation of Stalin. For most *linke Yidn*, the final break did not occur until 1967-68, when the Soviet Union sided with the Arab states in the Six Day War and the Polish government launched an anti-Semitic campaign under the guise of "anti-Zionism." But they retained a left wing orientation—non-communist, albeit not anti-communist— and a commitment to preserve Yiddish culture in various ways, including the translation project.

For example, in 1967 and 1995 respectively, the Sholem Aleichem Club of Philadelphia, Pennsylvania, which is both an educational and a cultural organization, published two volumes of Max Rosenfeld's translations of Yiddish short stories about Jewish life in America, *Pushcarts and Dreamers* and *New Yorkish*, the latter in partnership with the Congress of Secular Jewish Organizations (CSJO), a network of progressive secular Jewish Sunday schools and adult societies founded in 1970, of which the Sholem Aleichem Club is a member. The CSJO, a small entity with meager resources, also published *Apples and Honey: Music and Readings for a Secular Jewish Observance of the Jewish New Year Festival* (1995), which includes many humanistic Yiddish poems in English translation. In 1997, it published my pamphlet, *A Yiddish Short Story Sampler*, a much shorter version of this guide. To the best of my knowledge, no other resource of this nature existed then—or does any resource akin to it exist at the present time.

In 1989, the Zhitlovsky Foundation for Jewish Culture, led by Itche Goldberg, helped fund *A Century of Yiddish Poetry*, an anthology edited and translated by Aaron Kramer who made it a point to include the "Proletpen" poets of the communist left. In 1991, the Zhitlovsky Foundation published a bilingual collection of Peretz's stories edited and translated by Eli Katz.

In Canada, the Jewish magazine *Outlook*, established in 1963 as *Canadian Jewish Outlook*, with the same roots as *Jewish Currents*, continues to feature Yiddish poetry and prose in translation and the original Yiddish. Other Canadian periodicals have published Yiddish translations, but none with the consistency or passion of *Outlook*.

Jewish socialists also played a significant role in the translation project. Irving Howe, the greatest anthologist of translated Yiddish literature, including short stories, poetry and essays, was a committed socialist, as was his collaborator, Yiddish poet Eliezer Greenberg. Together, they were responsible for the publication in 1953 of the now classic I.B.Singer story "Gimpel the Fool" in the liberal journal *Partisan Review*, translated by a young Saul Bellow and the seminal *A Treasury of Yiddish Stories* in the following year, as well as other anthologies. Greenberg also served as editor of *Di Tsukunft*, a Yiddish literary journal aligned with Jewish socialists. Joseph Leftwich, a British Jew, whose literary and scholarly anthologies from the Yiddish were published in the US, was a socialist, too.

The organized Jewish socialist movement in the US, however, was less active. The Workmen's Circle/*Arbeter Ring* did not publish much Yiddish literature in translation, apart from its noted series of four song books, by Chana and Joseph Mlotek, which included many Yiddish poems put to music. The only other translations to its credit are a collection of Sholem Aleichem's plays (1967), a single play by the same author, *The Jackpot (Dos Groyse Gevins)* (1989), translated by Barnett Zumoff, and a slender volume of Holocaust literature (1983) edited and translated by Yiddish scholar Elias Schulman.

Individual members of the Workmen's Circle/*Arbeter Ring*, however, have been Yiddish translators in other venues. Four-time Workmen's Circle President Barnett Zumoff has done numerous translations including Jacob Glatstein's Holocaust Poems, *I Keep Recalling* (1993 Ktav), *Songs to a Moonstruck Lady: Yiddish Poems by and about Women* (2005, Tsar Publications), two collections of short stories by Tsvi Eisenman (2001, 2008, Ktav) and most recently *Yiddish Literature in America* (2009, Ktav) an anthology of essays, short stories, essays and poetry. Marvin Zuckerman, a Workmen's Circle leader and Yiddish educator from Southern California, has translated Mendele, Peretz and Sholem Aleichem.

In 2005 the Workmen's Circle became the publisher of *Jewish Currents*, the culmination of a grand reconciliation between the former pro-communist and social democratic branches of the Jewish left. Since 2004, *Jewish Currents* has included a regular bilingual Yiddish poetry column, *Mameloshn*, conducted by Zumoff, and has published numerous articles about Yiddish. Its unique contribution to Yiddish literature in translation was the 2007 publication in pamphlet form of a new translation of a Sholem Aleichem story, "Pity for Living Creatures," translated by Gerald Stillman, to accompany a Sholem Aleichem bobble-head doll. This story also appeared in the March/April 2009 issue. For financial reasons, Workmen's Circle has stopped publishing *Jewish Currents*. *Jewish Currents* re-emerged as an independent magazine with its May/June 2009 issue, its devotion to *yidishkayt* intact.

YIVO, the Yiddish Research Institute, founded in Vilna, Poland in 1925 and re-located to New York in 1940, has published outstanding scholarship in Yiddish and English, but only two translations of Yiddish fiction: a bi-lingual collection of Peretz stories (1947, Sol Liptzin) and *Yiddish Folktales* (in collaboration with Pantheon Books, 1988, Leonard Wolf.). Its longtime leader, Max Weinreich (1894-1969), the teacher of a generation of new Yiddish speakers and writers in the US, was a Bundist in his youth, and remained the model of a secular Jew. In Europe YIVO had ties with the Bund, but for many decades, it has been non-political.

One of the greatest proponents of Yiddish literature in translation today is the National Yiddish Book Center (NYBC), which has been non-political from its beginnings in 1980. Every issue of its quarterly journal *Pakn Treger* includes a bilingual short story. In 1995, in collaboration with a public radio station in California, the NYBC produced *Jewish Short Stories From Eastern Europe and Beyond*, nine cassette tapes (since converted into CDs) consisting of 31 short stories, 20 of them from the Yiddish. Other projects of this nature have followed, including an English CD of Sholem Aleichem's *Mottel the Cantor's Son*. However, in his superb book *Outwitting History*, NYBC founder Aaron Lansky reveals that most of the Center's major *zamlers* (book collectors) and supporters, in its formative years, were secular leftist Jews. He aptly describes Yiddish literature as "a counter culture" that presents "a challenge to mainstream values."

Of course, many Jews not identified with the secular Jewish left have produced major translations of Yiddish literature into English. (Maurice Samuel, Curt Leviant, Hillel Halkin, Ruth Wisse just to name a few). Not to be overlooked, *Midstream* devoted its entire July/August 2002 issue to "Yiddish Culture, Language and Literature," and has since included Yiddish-related material, including literary translations, in every July/August issue.

Among commercial publishers in the US, the pioneer was Alfred A. Knopf, the son of German Jewish immigrants. In 1920, he published the very first translation of Sholem Aleichem stories in the U.S., *Jewish Children* (1920, Hannah Berman), and all of I.J. Singer's translated novels, beginning with *The Brothers Ashkenazi* (1936, Maurice Samuel). Knopf published the first I.B. Singer novel that appeared in English, *The Family Moskat* (1950, A.H. Gross). During the 1980s, it published hardcover editions of Chaim Grade's *My Mother's Sabbath Days* (Chana Kleinerman Goldstein and Inna Hecker Grade) and *Rabbis and Wives* (Harold Rabinowitz and Inna Hecker Grade).

Thomas Yoseloff, the son of Russian Jewish immigrants, left a bigger impression. He published a significant number of Yiddish translations under multiple imprints, including Peretz (1958 and 1959, translated by Moshe Spiegel and Joseph Leftwich, respectively), Sholem Aleichem (1959, Curt Leviant), and three Mendele novels: *The Nag* (1955, Moshe Spiegel) *The Parasite* (1956, Gerald Stillman), and *Fishke the Lame* (1960, Gerald Stillman). Yoseloff also published the original 1963 edition of Ruth Rubin's *Voices of a People*, and an updated version of *The Golden Peacock* (1961), Joseph Leftwich's famous Yiddish poetry anthology, as well as others of Leftwich's contributions to Yiddish literature and scholarship.In the pre-modern realm, Thomas Yoseloff published a translation (by Beth-Zion Abrahams, 1963) of Glückel of Hameln's memoirs, *The Life of Glückel of Hameln.*

Farrar, Straus and Giroux, another Jewish-owned literary house, published nearly the entirety of I.B. Singer's works, while Crown, founded by Nat Wartels, also Jewish, published Sholem Aleichem's *The Old Country* (1946, Julius and Frances Butwin), *Tevye's Daughters* (1949, Frances Butwin), and *Wandering Stars* (1952, Frances Butwin), as well as Nathan Ausubel's *A Treasury of Jewish Folklore*. Between 1991 and 1996, Joseph Simon/Pangloss Press, a small Jewish publisher from California, produced a multi-volume series, *The Three Great Classic Writers of Modern Yiddish Literature*, consisting of Selected Works of Mendele Moykher-Sforim (Marvin Zuckerman, Gerald Stillman, Marion Herbst), Sholem Aleichem's *Tevye the Dairyman* (Miriam Katz, Marvin Zuckerman), and *Selected Works of I.L. Peretz* (Marvin Zuckerman, Marion Herbst).

A non-Jewish publisher, G.P.Putnam's Sons, released nearly all of Sholem Asch's novels and short story collections (the translators included Willa and Edwin Muir, Elsa Krauch, A.H. Gross, and Maurice Samuel) and six volumes of Sholem Aleichem's novels and short stories, from 1969 to 1985, including *The Adventures of Menahem-Mendel* (Tamara Kahan), *Old Country Tales* (Curt Leviant), and *In the Storm* (Aliza Shevrin).

As a publisher of Yiddish literature in English, Schocken Books was, until the turn of the 21st century, in a class by itself. Founded by Zalman Schocken (1877-1959), a secular liberal Zionist, its sole mission has been to promote Jewish studies. With *Inside Kasrilevke* (1948, Isidor Goldstick), Shocken became the third commercial publisher to translate Sholem Aleichem. A year later, it published Mendele's *The Travels and Adventures of Benjamin the Third* (Moishe Spiegel). Yiddish folksongs were well represented in Ruth Rubin's *A Treasury of Jewish Folksongs* (1950), and Yiddish folktales in Louis Newman's *Hasidic Anthology* (1963). Schocken also published I.J. Singer's *Family Carnovsky* (1969, Joseph Singer), and nearly all of Howe and Greenberg's translations of Yiddish literature in either hardcover or softcover editions, including the first paperback edition of the seminal *A Treasury of Yiddish Short Stories* (1973). In 1977, it published a soft cover edition of the Yiddish classic, *The Memoirs of Glückel of Hameln* (first translated in 1932 by Marvin Lowenthal). Schocken also produced the soft cover edition of Lucy Dawidowicz's indispensable *The Golden Tradition, Jewish Life and Thought in Eastern Europe* (1967).

In 1987, Schocken published softcover versions of Grade's *My Mother's Sabbath Days* (Chana Kleinerman Goldstein and Inna Hecker Grade) and *Rabbis and Wives* (Harold Rabinowiz and Inna Hecker Grade). In the same year, it inaugurated its *Library of Jewish Classics* with the issuance of Sholem Aleichem's *Tevye the Dairyman and the Railroad Stories* (Hillel Halkin), followed by *The I.L. Peretz Reader* (1990, Ruth Wisse) and Ansky's *The Dybbuk and Other Writings* (1992, translated mostly by Golda Werman). In 1996, Schocken issued Mendele's *Tales of Mendele the Book Peddler* (Dan Miron and Ted Gorelick).

The New Yiddish Library of Yale University has also issued editions of the same Peretz and Ansky titles published by Schocken, as well as Sholem Aleichem's *Letters of Menakhem Mendel* and *Motl the Cantor's Son* (2002, Hillel Halkin) and *The World According to Itsik—Selected Poetry and Prose of Itsik Manger* (2002, Leonard Wolf). In 2007, it published a novel, *Everyday Jews* by Yehoshue Perle (Maier Deshell and Margaret Birstein), and stories by Lamed Shapiro. Both Yale's New Yiddish Library and Schocken's Library of Jewish Classics series are joint projects of the National Yiddish Book Center and the Fund for the Translation of Yiddish Literature, which has received financial support from Felix Posen, a British Jewish philanthropist who endows universities to teach courses in secular Judaism.

Among university presses, Syracuse University has been most active at Yiddish translation, thanks in large part to Ken Frieden, a progressive secular Jew and professor, who is the editor of its *Judaic Traditions in Literature, Music and Arts* series and a translator in his own right. It has published works by Mendele, *The Wishing Ring* (2003, Michael Wex) and Sholem Aleichem (*Nineteen to the Dozen: Monologues and Bits and Bobs of Other Things*, (1998, Ted Gorelick); and *The Further Adventures of Menachem Mendel*, (2001, Aliza Shevrin). Peretz was added to the mix in Frieden's 2004 anthology, *Classic Yiddish Stories* (Ken Frieden, Ted Gorelick, and Michael Wex). Syracuse has also published works by S. Ansky (2000, Joachim Neugroschel), Dovid Bergelson (1996, Golda Werman) and Kadya Molodowsky (2006, Leah Schoolnik) and two novels by Chava Rosenfarb, *Bociany* and *Lodz and Love* (2000, both translated by the author). In 2001, Syracuse published an abridged edition of *The New Country: Stories from the Yiddish About Life in America* (originally published by YKUF), and in 2003, a bilingual edition of *The Jewish Book of Fables: The Selected Works of Eliezer Shtaynbarg* (Curt Leviant).

Yiddish continues to attract Jewish rebels and outsiders. Feminist, gay and lesbian Jews, for example, are among today's most passionate advocates for Yiddish culture. Irena Klepfisz, a Yiddish poet and translator, is the daughter of a Bundist who fell in the Warsaw Ghetto Uprising. She is a graduate of Workmen's Circle/

Arbeter Ring *shuln* (Yiddish schools), studied under Max Weinreich and received a degree in Yiddish from City College. A feminist and a lesbian, she provided the introduction and some of the translations for the first anthology of Yiddish women writers, *Found Treasures* (1994) and in 1995, she coordinated a conference entitled *Di Froyen* (The Women): Women and Yiddish.

Frieda Forman, the lead editor of *Found Treasures*, the first anthology of Yiddish women writers, although not secular, considers herself a progressive Jewish feminist. *Bridges: A Jewish Feminist Journal* founded in 1989, has as its "Yiddish editor" Faith Jones, a gay feminist and secular Jew, who has translated Yiddish poetry into English. She is also a regular contributor to *Outlook*, Canada's secular Jewish progressive magazine. *Rhea Tregebov*, editor of the second anthology of Yiddish fiction by women, *Arguing with the Storm: Stories by Yiddish Women Writers* (2007), is a progressive secular Jewish feminist from Canada.

The Dora Teitelboim Center for Yiddish Culture, named after the leftist Jewish poet of the same name, collaborated with the University of Wisconsin Press in the publication of *Proletpen: America's Rebel Yiddish Poets* (Amelia Glaser, 2005), an anthology of leftwing poets that includes Teitelboim. It also nurtured the publication of twelve other translations, mainly poetry collections including Teitelboim's, *All My Yesterdays Were Steps* (KTAV, 1995, Aaron Kramer) and *Songs to a Moonstruck Lady* (Tsar Publications, 2006, Barnett Zumoff) as well as *Inheritance (Yerushe)* by Peretz Markish (Tsar Publications, 2007, Mary Shulman). Working with the Syracuse University Press, the Center shepherded the publication of *The Last Butterfly* (1998) consisting of Holocaust poetry translated by Aaron Kramer, *The Jewish Book of Fables: The Selected Works of Eliezer Shtaynbarg* (2003, Curt Leviant) and a prose collection—an abridged edition of *The New Country: Stories About Jewish Life in America* (2001). A number of these poetry collections appear in bi-lingual editions. Notably, David Weintraub, the Executive Director of the Center and a co-editor of both *Proletpen* and the Markish collection, identifies as a secular progressive Jew.

It is clear that these Jews consider Yiddish as a counter culture.

So do the editors of the three of the most recent anthologies of Yiddish literature in translation, *Beautiful As the Moon, Radiant as the Stars: Jewish Women in Yiddish Stories* (2003), edited by Martha Bark; *Prophets & Dreamers: A Selection of Great Yiddish Literature* (2002), edited by Miriam Weinstein; and *No Star Too Beautiful: Yiddish Stories from 1382 to the Present* (2002), edited by Joachim Neugroschel, a gay man, who has edited three related anthologies as well.

The latest anthology, *Yiddish in America 1870-2000* (Ktav, 2009) consists mainly of poetry and essays, with a few short stories. Its editor, Emanuel Goldsmith, is a Reconstructionist rabbi; its translator the aforementioned Barnett Zumoff, a leader in the secular progressive Jewish world for decades.

Although literacy in Yiddish is diminishing, there is still considerable interest in reading the original among academics, college students and Yiddish book clubs/reading circles (*leyen krayzn*). The International Association of Yiddish Clubs, made up of older Jews who read and speak Yiddish at various levels of proficiency, still thrives and pockets of younger Jews have been attracted to *mameloshn*—the mother tongue of their ancestors. *Di Tsukunft* (The Future), *Afn Shvel* (On the Threshhold) and *Yugntruf* (The Call of Youth) survive as Yiddish literary journals and have recently been joined by *Gilgulim* (Reincarnated Souls).

How accessible is Yiddish literature to North American Jews? For the overwhelming majority that do not read Yiddish and the few that do, *Yiddish Stories For Young People* is a great resource to introduce children to the joys of Yiddish literature in translation, but it is out of print. The children's stories of the two most popular Yiddish writers, Sholem Aleichem and I.B. Singer, are available in translation, but outside of the relatively small number of secular Jewish Sunday school programs, they are probably not used much. In religious Sunday or day schools, Yiddish literature in any form is generally neglected, because their curriculum is based on Hebrew, Israel and religious instruction.

For adults, it is all well and good to send someone to the library for a book by a translated Yiddish author, and it is true that a number of excellent collections of Yiddish stories in translation are available, especially Irving Howe and Eliezer Greenberg's classic *A Treasury of Yiddish Stories* (1954). However, it remains a daunting task for interested readers, burdened by a heavy load of work, family, communal and other responsibilities, to gain an appreciation for Yiddish literature without specific guidance. Students studying Yiddish literature in translation in universities no doubt receive guidance from their professors, but they too could benefit a systematic treatment of the subject.

At a minimum, it is my hope that this guide prompts Jews interested in Yiddish literature, including teachers, students and Yiddish clubs, to study these stories in the original or in translation and use them in academic courses and adult education programs. With a little creativity, they can find their way into holiday or life cycle celebrations. Strange as it may sound, this is the only resource of its kind in existence.

For those who read Yiddish or are learning Yiddish, this guide provides the Yiddish title and source for all the stories. There is one bilingual collection listed in the bibliography and others referenced in this introduction. So where can most Yiddish books be found? Those living in metropolitan New York have it easiest. YIVO's library is the mother lode (212-246-6080) but the New York Public Library's Dorot Jewish Division (212-930-0971) also has an extensive Yiddish collection.

Other repositories of Yiddish literature include the Library of Congress in Washington D.C, the Klau Library (Hebrew Union College) in Cincinnati and various large university libraries. In Canada, McGill University in Montreal and the University of Toronto's Robarts Library have the best Yiddish collections. And there is always the internet, especially the Mendele website at www2.trincoll.edu/~mendele

A brave new world in Yiddish has emerged since the National Yiddish Book Center in Amherst, MA digitized its entire collection of 1.5 million Yiddish books so that they can be reprinted and purchased on demand. Eleven thousand of these titles can also be read for free on line. (Go to www.bikher.org).

There are 135 stories summarized in this guide and they are organized by topic and by holiday. Most of the stories themselves do not exceed 15 pages or so. It is safe to assume that shorter stories are more likely to be read—and used. My criteria for selecting certain stories over others may be questioned by some, but readers should expect to find summaries of a solid core of the best Yiddish short stories, as recognized by literary critics and scholars in the field, as well as lesser known stories of genuine interest. A special effort was made to reference stories by and about women. Finally, I took the liberty of including some chapters of novels and excerpts from memoirs.

Sources for introduction

The Canadian Jewish Outlook Anthology. Rosenthal, Henry and Berson, S. Cathy, eds. Vancouver: New Star Books, 1988.

Commentary Reader—Two Decades of Articles and Stories. Norman Podhoretz, ed. New York: Atheneum, 1967.

"Jewish Currents" Reader, 1956-1966. New York: Jewish Currents, 1966.

A Ten Year Harvest—Third Decennial Reader, 1966-1976. Harap, Louis, ed. New York: Jewish Currents, 1977.

Jewish Currents Reader 4, 1976-1986. Harap, Louis, ed. New York: Jewish Currents, 1987.

Jewish Frontier Anthology, 1935-1945. New York: Jewish Frontier Association, 1945.

Jewish Frontier Anthology, 1945-1967. New York: Jewish Frontier Association, 1967.

"Jewish Life" Anthology, 1946-1956. New York: Jewish Life, 1956.

The Menorah Treasury—Harvest of Half a Century, Schwarz, Leo, ed. Philadelphia: Jewish Publication Society, 1964.

Midstream Reader, Katz, Shlomo, ed.. New York: Thomas Yoseloff, 1960.

Abramowicz, Dina. **Yiddish Literature in English Translation: List of Books in Print.** New York: YIVO, 1968, 1969, 1976.

Ausubel, Nathan. **Jewish Culture in America: Weapon for Jewish Survival and Progress.** New York: New Century Publishers, 1948.

Buhle, Paul; Buhle, Mari Jo; Georgakas, Dan. **Encyclopedia of the American Left.** Champaign, Illinois: University of Illinois Press, 1992 (various articles on the Yiddish left).

Denman, Hugh. "Anthologies of Yiddish Literature," *Mendele Review* (on-line journal), Vol. 08.008, July 29, 2004.

Glaser, Amelia and Weintraub, David. **Proletpen: America's Rebel Yiddish Poets.** Madison: University of Wisconsin Press, 2005.

Katz, Dovid. **Words on Fire: The Unfinished Story of Yiddish.** New York: Basic Books, 2004.

Lansky, Aaron. **Outwitting History—The Amazing Adventures of the Man Who Rescued a Million Yiddish Books.** Chapel Hill, N.C.: Algonquin Books, 2005.

Parker, Sandra, "An Educational Assessment of the Yiddish Secular School Movements in the United States," p.295-312 in Fishman, Joshua A, **Never Say Die—A Thousand Years of Yiddish in Jewish Life and Letters,** The Hague: Mouton Publishers, 1980.

Roback, A. A. **The Story of Yiddish Literature.** New York: YIVO, 1940.

Sachar, Howard. **A History of the Jews in America.** New York: Vintage, 1993 .

Shandler, Jeffrey, "Anthologizing the Vernacular: Collections of Yiddish Literature in English Translation," p.304-323 in Stern, David, **The Anthology in Yiddish Literature,** New York: Oxford University Press, 2004.

e-mail correspondence and/or phone interviews with Frieda Forman, Ken Frieden, Troim Katz Handler, Rhea Tregebov, David Weintraub and Marvin Zuckerman.

Stories for All Seasons

Questioning God's Justice

Three Gifts by I.L. Peretz
Yiddish title: **Dray Matones**

To gain entrance to heaven, a Jewish soul must present the saints in Paradise with three gifts that are "extraordinarily beautiful and good." These gifts turn out to be symbols of Jewish martyrdom. While Jews on earth are willing to die to defend their beliefs, God appears indifferent to their suffering.

*Ruth Wisse, ed., The I.L. Peretz Reader, p.222-230; and
Miriam Weinstein, ed., Prophets & Dreamers, p.47-54.
Yiddish source: Ale Verk—Y.L. Perets, 1:13-24, Vilna 1925-29.*

Berl the Tailor by I.L. Peretz
Yiddish title: **Berl Der Shnayder**

The famous Hasidic *rebbe*, Levi Yitzkhok of Berditchev, summons a man who is absent from *shul* (synagogue) on Yom Kippur and invites him to state his complaint against God. The man, a poor tailor, tells how he landed a good job sewing a fur coat for a rich landlord and smuggled out some left over pelts in a loaf of bread. He hid the bread in a safe place, but when he went to retrieve it, it was gone. He is convinced that God made it disappear to punish him for stealing. Because God has taken pains to doom him to a life of grinding poverty, the tailor has repudiated God and His laws. That is why he did not come to *shul* on Yom Kippur. He will only return to the faith if God forgives "sins" such as his. The congregation is ready to tear the tailor to bits for his heresy, but the *rebbe* takes the tailor's side, communes with God and informs the tailor that he "won." The tailor then rejoins the congregation.

Eli Katz, ed., Yitskhok Leybush Peretz, Selected Stories—Bi-lingual Edition (Geklibene Dertseylungen), p.214-227.

Today's Children by Sholem Aleichem
Yiddish title: **Hayntike Kinder**

In two brief excerpts from **Tevye the Dairyman**, the basis for *Fiddler on the Roof*, Tevye reveals the resentment and anger that lurk beneath his piety. He complains to God for bringing him misfortune and tolerating a society full of social injustice. In the end, he resigns himself to the status quo, but his questions remain unanswered.

Sholem Aleichem, Tevye the Dairyman and the Railroad Stories, p.45-47; and Tevye's Daughters (Modern Children), p.20-38.
Yiddish source: Tevye Der Milkhiker, AV' 42, Band 5, Giml: 67-91.

Night by Elie Wiesel (See **The Holocaust**)

Ethics and Piety

Rabbi Yochanan the Warden by I.L. Peretz
Yiddish title: **Reb Yoykenen Gabe**

An exemplary rabbi believes he has done the right thing by closing the *shul* at night to keep out beggars, but as a consequence, a beggar freezes to death. Both men die and are summoned to a heavenly court. Which one will be judged righteous?

Irving Howe and Eliezer Greenberg, eds,. A Treasury of Yiddish Stories, p.243-245.
Yiddish source: Ale Verk—Y.L. Perets, vol. 4, NY: Farlag "Idish," 1920.

At the Head of a Dying Man by I.L. Peretz
Yiddish title: **Baym Goyses Tsukopns**

In the second half of this famous story, a dying Jew who neglected many of the religious commandments, but who devoted his life to helping the unfortunate, is offered the opportunity to enter Paradise. He chooses to go to Hell, where he can share in the suffering of the damned.

Eli Katz, ed., Y.L. Peretz Selected Stories (Geklibene Dertseylungen), p.184-191; and Itche Goldberg, ed., Yiddish Stories for Young People, p.115-122.

The Tallis Koton by Sholem Aleichem
Yiddish title: **Tales Kotn**

Written in the inimitable style of the master satirist, this tale relates how two Jews, one a rascal, the other a heretic, join forces to trick a miserly religious hypocrite into donating money to a relief fund for victims of a fire.

Sholem Aleichem, Tevye the Dairyman and the Railroad Stories, p.199-207; and Sholem Aleichem, Old Country Tales (Ritual Fringes), p.226-233.
Yiddish source: Ayzn Ban Geshikhtes: Ksovim Fun A Komivoyazher, AV'42, Band 5, Hey: 141-151.

In the Synagogue by Chaim Grade
(from the novella **Leybe-Leyzer's Courtyard**)
Yiddish title: **none**

A pious Jewish student refuses to interrupt a prayer service to speak with his poor mother, who travelled a great distance to see him. Her mother leaves and before he takes the time to return home, she dies with "My son is a saint!" on her lips.

Emanuel Goldsmith, Yiddish Literature in America 1870-2000, p.328-331 and Chaim Grade, Rabbis and Wives, p. 215-218
Yiddish source: Leybe-Leyzer's Hoyf

Passions (an excerpt) by Isaac Bashevis Singer
Yiddish title: **Tayves**

A poor uneducated tailor reacts to an insult he receives from a rich man in front of their entire congregation by swearing that in one year he will become more learned than the rich man himself. The stakes are a house the rich man promises to build for the poor man and a fur coat the poor man promises to sew for the rich man's wife. The tailor devotes the next year to study, and to the delight of the poor people in town, is judged the superior scholar. But rather than profit from his glory, he donates the house to the community for public use and returns to his life as a tailor.

The Collected Stories of Isaac Bashevis Singer, p.488-493.
Yiddish source: the journal Di Goldene Keyt, 87, 1975.

The Redemption of Captives by A. S. Sachs aka Zaks
Yiddish title: **Di Kalpi**

A poor shoemaker, who takes it upon himself to ensure that Jewish prisoners receive kosher meals on the Sabbath, does a far greater service to the community than its most pious members.

A.S. Sachs, Worlds That Passed, p.91-98; and Azriel Eisenberg, ed., Modern Jewish Life in Literature, Book 1 (Simon the Shoemaker, First Citizen), p.55-57.
Yiddish source: Khoreve Veltn, kapitl 14, Literarisher ferlag, New York, 1917.

Obsolescence by David Bergelson
Yiddish title: **Altvarg**

The children of an old pious Jewish widower find him a new wife, but soon send her away and obtain a divorce because she is peculiar. The old man feels very guilty for not fulfilling the religious obligation to ask her forgiveness, but lacks the will to act. Instead he spends all his time reading the holy books and regretting the past. Yet he too has suffered. He was uprooted from his home and traditional life in the Ukraine by the Russian Revolution and is alienated from his new surroundings in a big city.

Midstream, July/August 2000, p.39-42.
Yiddish source: the short story collection, Shturemteg, Kiev,1927, reprinted in Dertseylungen (Collected Works), Vilna, 1930.

Avrom Leyb the Shoemaker by Kadya Molodowsky
Yiddish title: **Avrom Leyb Der Shuster**

A humble shoemaker struggles for the honor of repairing the shoes of the town's schoolchildren free of charge—and is honored in return with an *aliyah* on Rosh Hashana.

Kayda Molodowsky, A House With Seven Windows, p.263-268.
Yiddish source: A Shtub Mit Zibn Fentster, New York, 1957.

Life in the Shtetl
(the unromantic view)

The Exchange by Mendele Mocher Seforim
Yiddish title: **Der Khilef**

An episode from the life of a Jewish bookseller in Old Russia, involving a dead horse, a case of mistaken identity and a Passover seder, as told in the ironic style of the founder of modern Yiddish literature.

Joseph Leftwich, ed., Yisroel: The First Jewish Omnibus, p.416-422.
Yiddish source: Sholem Abramovitsh, Ale Verk fun Mendele Moykher-Sforim, vol. 16, Shabes un Yontef, Warsaw: Farlag Mendele, 1928.

A Nap, Prayers and Strawberries by
Mendele Mocher Seforim (excerpt from a novel)
Yiddish title: none

Mendele the bookseller struggles to resist worldly temptations on a beautiful summer day that happens to be a holiday that calls for fasting and lamentation.

Leo Schwarz, ed., Feast of Leviathan, p.159-66; Marvin Zuckerman, Gerald Stillman, Marion Herbst, Selected Works of Mendele Moykher-Sforim, Fishke the Lame, p.174-84; and Miriam Weinstein, ed. Prophets & Dreamers, p.20-30.
Yiddish source: Fishke der Krumer, kapitln 1-2, Sholem Y. Abramovitsh, Ale Verk fun Mendele Moykher Sforim, Band 12, New York, 1911-1913.

The Pious Cat by I.L. Peretz
Yiddish: **Di Frume Kats**

An allegory about the destructive effects of religious fanaticism.

Wisse, The I.L. Peretz Reader, p.128-130; and Eli Katz, Y. L. Peretz Selected Stories (Geklibene Dertseylungen), p.118-125.

What is Soul? The Story of a Young Man by I.L Peretz
Yiddish title: **Vos Heyst Neshome?**

An orphaned young man, suspected of being a freethinker, is allowed to marry the girl of his dreams only because he lacks sufficient standing in the community to warrant a "better" match. This story also reveals Peretz' opinion of what passed for education in the shtetl: Ignorant teachers teach restless boys superstitious nonsense, with the help of their favorite method—corporal punishment.

Wisse, The I.L. Peretz Reader, p.93-104.
Yiddish source: Dertseylungen, Ale Verk—Y.L. Perets, Volume 3, New York: Farlag "Idish," 1920.

The Shtrayml by I.L. Peretz
Yiddish title: **Dos Shtrayml**

A poor Jewish tailor who typically makes coats for Gentile peasants and Jewish workers, takes perverse pleasure in sewing a fur hat for a Hasidic *rebbe* because of the vast power wielded by the *rebbe* over the community in the enforcement of oppressive rituals.

Ken Frieden, Classic Yiddish Stories of S.Y. Abramovitsh, Sholem Aleichem and I.L. Peretz, p.138-146.
Yiddish source: Literature un lebn: a zamlbukh far literature un gezelshaft, Warsaw, 1894, p.119-134.

Bandits by Sholem Aleichem
Yiddish title: **Gazlonim**

On Lag Boymer, aka "the scholar's holiday," school boys take their revenge on a tyrannical teacher, but later regret it.

Howe and Wisse, The Best of Sholem Aleichem, p.271-280; and Aliza Shevrin, A Treasury of Sholom Aleichem Children's Stories, p.317-328.
Yiddish source: Lekoved Yontif, Tsveyter Bukh, AV'42 Band 1, Daled 147-160.

Two Shalachmones or a Purim Scandal by Sholem Aleichem
Yiddish title: **Tsvey Shalekhmonesn**

When two hungry servant girls eat up the *shalachmones* meant for each other's employers, nasty accusations fly between the two families. A wise rabbi shames the feuding parties by reminding them of their obligation as Jews to "love thy neighbor as thyself." The families reconcile, but the servants are not forgiven.

Sholem Aleichem, Tevye's Daughters, p.193-202; and Shevrin, A Treasury of Sholom Aleichem Children's Stories (Two Purim Pastry Gifts), p.279-293.
Yiddish source: Kleyne Mentshelekh Mit Kleyne Hasoges, AV'42, Band 5, Beys: 87-103.

The Merrymakers by Sholem Aleichem
Yiddish title: **Me Hulyet**

In this poignant vignette, three poor Jews forget their troubles on Simkhes Toyre by drinking and carousing. But what do they really have to celebrate?

Sholem Aleichem, Tevye's Daughters, p.162-171.
Yiddish source: Oreme Un Freylekhe: Tsveyter Bukh, AV' 42, Band 4, Daled: 227-259.

Tit for Tat by Sholem Aleichem
Yiddish title: **Vort Far a Vort**

The Village of Habne by Sholem Aleichem
Yiddish title: **Khabne**
In both stories, practical jokers drive the point home that the shtetl elite, i.e., the rabbis and the *balebatim* ("respectable citizens"), were not always to be trusted.

Sholem Aleichem, The Old Country, p.200-217 and Old Country Tales, p.302-313.
Yiddish source: Vort Far a Vort: Fun Kasrilevke, AV'42 Band 4, Alef 147-168; and Khabne: Monologn, AV'42 Band 3, Daled: 137-151.

The Factory by Abraham Reisin
Yiddish title: **Di Fabrik**
Schoolboys are fascinated by the construction of a factory in their town until they discover that it has polluted their swimming hole.

Avrom Reisen, Poor Matza, p. 37-45
Yiddish source: Geklibene Dertseylungen un Lider, Education Department of the Workmen's Circle, 1947, p. 37-42

No More Rabbi by Sarah Hamer-Jacklyn
Yiddish title: **Oys Rebe**

A young girl who makes a special effort to satisfy the hunger of her baby boy cousin is chastised and ostracized because she turned to a Gentile woman to nurse him.

Rhea Tregebov, Arguing with the Storm: Stories by Yiddish Women Writers, p.45-54; and Pakn Treger, Spring 2008/5768, Number 56, p.38-42.
Yiddish source: Shtamen un Tsvaygn: Dertseylungen, Promotion Press, New York, 1954; and Pakn Treger, Spring 2008/5768, Number 56, p. 37-43.

A Tale of a Goat by I.M. Weissenberg
Yiddish title: **A Mayse Mit a Tsig**

Superstition and hypocrisy rule the shtetl in this comic tale.

Joachim Neugroschel,ed., The Shtetl: a creative anthology of Jewish Life in Eastern Europe, p.451-458.
Yiddish source: A. M. Vaysenberg, Gezamlte Shriftn, Literarisher farlag, NY, 1919, also Geklibene Verk, Chicago: Zelechow Society of the World, 1959.

Electricity (an excerpt from a novel) by Moshe Kulbak
Yiddish title: **Elektre**

Electricity comes to a shtetl in the Soviet Union. Despite its obvious benefits, it receives a cool reception from the townspeople.

Irving Howe and Eliezer Greenberg, Ashes Out of Hope: Fiction by Soviet Yiddish Writers, p.144-153.
Yiddish source: the novel, Zelmenyaner, Geklibene Verk, CYCO, NY, 1953.

Apikorsim and Other "Heretics"

My Quarrel with Hersh Rasseyner by Chaim Grade
Yiddish title: **Mayn Krig Mit Hersh Raseyner**

An epic confrontation between Jewish secularism and ortho-
doxy. Two Holocaust survivors living in Paris debate radically op-
posing views of Jewish identity and values.

Howe and Greenberg, A Treasury of Yiddish Stories, p.579-606.
Yiddish source: the journal, Der Yidisher Kemfer, Sept. 28, 1951, p.33-44.

I Enlighten a Shtetl by S. Ansky
Yiddish title: **Hattos Ne'urim**
In this memoir of a Yiddish writer's early years as a *maskil*, i.e.
a modernist, his attempt to introduce the ideas of the *Haskalah*
(Jewish Enlightenment) to a shtetl, arouses a furious reaction from
the rabbi and the leading townspeople.

*Lucy Dawidowicz, ed., The Golden Tradition—Jewish Life and Thought
in Eastern Europe, p.307-311; and Ansky, S. The Dybbuk and Other
Writings (The Sins of Youth).*
*Yiddish source: Zikhroynes, Part I, Warsaw. 1925, p.5-15 and Gezamalte
Shriftn: New York, 1920-25, vol. 10, p.5-16.*

A Boy Philosopher by Isaac Bashevis Singer
Yiddish title: **A Yingl A Filosof**

In this memoir. a young I. B. Singer witnesses a debate between
his older brother Israel Joseph, an *apikoris* (freethinker), and his
traditional parents over the place of Judaism among the world's
religions, the existence of God, the morality of the Bible—and
Isaac's own future.

In My Father's Court by Isaac Bashevis Singer, p.153-157.
Yiddish source: Mayn Tatn's Bezdn Shtub, 1954.

They Lived to Regret by Zalman Libin
Yiddish title: **Es Hoybt Zey On Tsu Ferdrisn**

In their early years together, a couple embrace anarchism, which they apply as a mandate to break social conventions and repudiate their Jewishness. Later in life they regret their decision and seek to instill Jewish pride in their school-aged child.

Henry Goodman, ed., The New Country, p.332-339.
Yiddish source: Gezamelte Verk, vol. 4, Forverts, New York, 1915, p.259-266.

A Yiddish Speaking Socialist by Zalman Libin
Yiddish title: **A Yiddish-Shprekhender Sotsyalist**
A radical who wonders whether he is just a "Yiddish speaking socialist" or a Jew, finds his answer when he seeks refuge from an anti-Semitic gang in a synagogue during Tisha B'Av and is moved to join in the service that mourns the tragedies that have befallen the Jewish people.

Albert Waldinger, Shining and Shadow: An Anthology of Early Yiddish Stories from the Lower East Side, p.70-73.
Yiddish source: Gezamelte Verk, vol.1, Forverts, New York, 1915, p.132-140.

The Curse of Poverty

Bontshe the Silent by I.L. Peretz
Yiddish title: **Bontshe Shvayg**

In this classic story, Peretz depicts a heavenly tribunal that judges the soul of a poor downtrodden Jew. Although the angels praise him as a saint and offer him all the rewards of Paradise, the man's miserable life on earth has so crushed his spirit that all he can bring himself to ask for is a hot roll with fresh butter every morning.

Wisse, The I.L. Peretz Reader, p.146-151; Howe and Greenberg, A Treasury of Yiddish Stories, p.223-230; and Weinstein, Prophets & Dreamers p.47-54.
Yiddish source: Eli Katz, Y.L. Peretz Selected Stories—Bilingual Edition (Geklibene Dertseylungen), p.192-213.

Three Little Heads by Sholem Aleichem
Yiddish title: Dray Keplekh

Small children living in urban poverty never experience the beauty of nature. The closest they come is the greenery their father brings home for Shevuos.

Sholem Aleichem, The Old Country, p.329-335.
Yiddish source: Oreme Un Freylekhe: Tsveyter Bukh, AV'42, Band 1, Daled: 135-143.

Matza for the Rich by Abraham Reisen
Yiddish title: Negidishe Matse

The workers in a bakery work twice as hard preparing matza for a rich matron in anticipation of generous tips, but they are sorely disappointed.

Abraham Reisen, The Heart-Stirring Sermon and Other Stories, p.91-102.
Yiddish source: Ale Verk fun Avrom Reyzin, vol. 8, Oreme Gemeyndn.

The Quiet Jubilee by Zalman Libin
Yiddish title: A Shtiler Yubileum

An immigrant celebrates ten years as a worker in America only to realize how many of his fellow workers did not survive the ordeal, and how he himself has become enslaved to a machine.

Henry Goodman, ed., The New Country, p.148-154.
Yiddish source: Gezamlte Verk, Forverts, New York, 1915, p.33-40.

The Hand of God by Boruch Glazman
Yiddish title: **Gots Hant**

A family of striking workers, with the wolf at the door, remain honest in the face of great temptation—and suffer for it. Where is justice in an unjust society?

Max Rosenfeld, New Yorkish and Other American Yiddish Stories, p.120-128.
Yiddish source: Ateneo Literario en el YIVO, Buenos Aires, vol. 86, 1981.

The Aunt from Norfolk by Bertha Lelchuk
Yiddish title: **Di Tante fun Norfolk**

A rich aunt visiting her poor relations in New York City prattles on about her petty problems, while ignoring their desperate situation and even adding to their burdens.

Joachim Neugroschel, ed., No Star Too Beautiful: Yiddish Stories from 1382 to the Present, p.620-624.
Yiddish source: Shtotns Oyf Der Zun, Signal, New York, 1938, p.11-17.

When Workers Organize

A Union for Shabbos by Sholem Asch
Yiddish title: **A Yunyon far Shabes**

Even Orthodox Jews become militant unionists when the boss insists that they work on the Sabbath.

Max Rosenfeld, ed., Pushcarts and Dreamers, p.83-89.
Yiddish source: Gezamelte Shriften, Amerike, Ferter Band, Tsveyter
Oysgabe, Sholem Asch Committee, 1923, p.162-167.

Chewing Gum (the story of a shop girl) by Abraham Reisen
Yiddish title: **Tshuing Gum (dertseylung fun a shop meydl)**

Young women working in a shop under an abusive boss are provoked to strike by the removal of a chewing gum vending machine.

Avrom Reisen, Poor Matza, p. 46-48
Yiddish source: Nyu-Yorker Noveln, B. Kletskin, Vilna, 1929, p. 272-
275

A Strike Meeting In the Synagogue by I. J. Singer
(an excerpt from a novel)
Yiddish title: none

Jewish weavers, exploited unmercifully by a Jewish factory own-
er in Poland, first pray in synagogue and then use the same space
as a meeting hall to call a strike. In drawing on Jewish tradition,
they compare themselves to slaves in Egypt and their boss to a
modern day Pharoah, and swear "by the Law of God" to remain
united until victory.

I. J. Singer, The Brothers Ashkenazi, p.158-170.
Yiddish source: Di Brider Ashkenazi (Kapitl 17), NY, Farlag Matones,
1951.

We are on Strike by Sholem Aleichem
Yiddish title: **Mir Straykn**

Seen from the playful perspective of a ten year old boy, Jewish
workers take on their abusive bosses in the New York City garment
industry

Sholem Aleichem, Adventures of Mottel, the Cantor's Son, p.283-292; The Letters of Menakhem Mendel and Sheyne Sheyndel and Motl the Cantor's Son (We're on Strike), p.284-288; and Goodman, The New Country (We Strike), p.85-91.
Yiddish source: Motl Peyse Dem Khazns: Tsveyter Teyl: In Amerike, AV'42, Band 1, Beys.

Kapores by Sholem Aleichem
Yiddish title: **same**

A parable: Chickens go on strike to abolish the sacrificial ceremony on Yom Kippur. By not allowing themselves to be divided, sticking to their principles and using militant tactics, they win.

Itche Goldberg, Yiddish Stories For Young People, p.57-71; and Aliza Shevrin, A Treasury of Sholem Aleichem's Children's Stories (No More Kapores or the Sacrificial Chicken Revolt), p.149-159.
Yiddish source: Mayses Far Yidishe Kinder: Ershter Bukh, AV'42, Band 1, Hey.

A Meal for the Poor by Mordecai Spector
Yiddish title: **A Shtrayk fun Kabtsonim**

In this parody, a crowd of beggars, full from feasting at a wedding, refuse to accept an invitation to be guests at a second wedding unless the founder of the feast pays them. For once they have "bargaining power." Their benefactor gives in to their demand and joyously fulfills the traditional obligation to serve the poor himself.

Howe and Greenberg, A Treasury of Yiddish Stories, p.250-255.
Yiddish source: Bikher far Ale #21, Ferlag "Bikher far Ale," Varshe Dluga 26, 1905.

Jews and the Military

Back from the Draft by Sholem Aleichem
Yiddish title: Funem Prizev

A Jewish father, caught in a maze of bureaucratic bungling, tries to extricate his only son from the draft. (Because of Russian anti-Semitism, most Jewish men would stop at nothing to avoid serving in the Czar's army.) Here the issue gets the comic treatment; sarcasm is directed toward Jews and Gentiles alike.

Sholem Aleichem, Old Country Tales, p.247-258; and Sholem Aleichem, Tevye the Dairyman and the Railroad Stories (The Automatic Exemption) p.229-238.
Yiddish source: Ayznban Geshikhtes: Ksovim Fun a Komivoyazher, AV'42, Band 5, Hey: 197-211.

The First Passover Night of the War by Sholem Aleichem
Yiddish title: Di Ershte Nakht Peysekh Oyf Der Milkhome

Sholem Aleichem adopts a different tone in this story of a Jew who is proud to be a Russian soldier. He stands up to one anti-Semitic soldier and wins the respect of the rest of his company.

Sholem Aleichem, Old Country Tales, p.259-265.
Yiddish source: Lekoved Yontif: Ershter Bukh, AV'42 Band 1, Giml: 107-117.

Gitl Purishkevitch by Sholem Aleichem
Yiddish title: same title

A poor but feisty Jewish widow challenges the corrupt practices in her town that cause her only son to be drafted while three rich boys receive exemptions. She takes her complaint all the way to St. Petersburg, the Russian capital—and after a prolonged struggle—and a great deal of kvetching—she wins!

Sholem Aleichem, Old Country Tales, p.139-148.
Yiddish source: Monologn, AV'42, Band 3, Daled: 223-234.

The Draft by Fishel Bimko
Yiddish title: **Biz Tsum Priziv**

Rich and poor Jewish youth have contrasting reactions to a draft call in Czarist Russia. Told from the perspective of urban "punks," this story is rated "R" for vulgar language and violence, revealing a neglected underside of Jewish life.

Neugroschel, The Shtetl: a creative anthology of Jewish life in Eastern Europe, p.471-480.
Yiddish source: Geklibene Verk, New York, 1947.

From Barrack and War (an excerpt from a novel) by Yankev Kreplak
Yiddish title: none

A Jewish soldier in the Czar's army seems to win the sympathy of his comrades when he confronts another soldier who tells how he once tortured a Jewish vagabond. However, he soon realizes that their sympathy for Jewish suffering would never cause them to come to the aid of a Jewish victim.

Neugroschel, No Star Too Beautiful, p.506-511.
Yiddish source: Fun Kazarme un Milkhome, New York, 1927.

Chasing After Villa by Abraham Reisen
Yiddish title: **Der Foter**

A Jewish father in the U.S. allows his son to join the army because it entitles him to certain government benefits, but has second thoughts when the boy is sent off to war. The "Villa" in this story is the Mexican revolutionary Pancho Villa whose cross-border raids provoked an American attack on Mexico in 1916.

Rosenfeld, Pushcarts and Dreamers, p.101-104; and Goodman, The New Country (The Father) p.233-236.
Yiddish source: Ale Verk fun Avrom Reyzin, Eynakters un Monologn, vol. 6, p.7-12.

Khurbn — The Holocaust

A Ghetto Dog by Isaiah Spiegel
Yiddish title: **Niki**

An old Jewish woman, who had distanced herself from other Jews, is rounded up by the Nazis along with her beloved dog and confined to a Jewish ghetto. There she is befriended by a Jewish prostitute. When the Nazis order all Jews to give up their pets, she wraps the leash around her arm as if it was *tfiln* (phylacteries) and refuses to be parted with her dog. She, her dog and hundreds of other ghetto dogs are then sent to their death.

Howe and Greenberg, A Treasury of Yiddish Stories, p.569-579.
Yiddish source: Shtern Laykhtn in Tom, Tel Aviv: 1976.

The Road of No Return by Rachel Korn
Yiddish title: **Der Letster Veg**
Trapped in a ghetto, a Jewish family is ordered to select one of its members to be turned over to the Nazis.
Forman et al., Found Treasures-Stories by Yiddish Women Writers, p.211-22.
Yiddish source: Nayn Dertseylungen, Montreal, 1957.

Night by Elie Wiesel
Yiddish title: see Yiddish source, below

While other Jews in Auschwitz pray on Rosh Hashana, the teenage Wiesel condemns God—and ten days later, he eats on

Yom Kippur, to defy Him.

Elie Wiesel, Night, p.63–66.
Yiddish source: from a much longer version, Un Di Velt Hot Geshvign (And the World Remained Silent) Buenos Aires, Argentina, 1956.

The Duty to Live by Sholem Asch
Yiddish title: **A Mitsve Tsu Lebn**

A twelve-year-old girl, following her mother's injunction to "preserve life," succeeds in saving herself and her two-year-old brother from the Nazis. Finding refuge at a convent, she shows the nuns her determination to remain Jewish by having her brother recite the first words of a Hebrew prayer.

Schwarz, ed., Feast of Leviathan, p.139–152; and Sholem Asch, Tales of My People, p.205–219.
Yiddish source (and longer original version): Der Brenendiker Dorn, Idisher Fraternaler Folks Ordn, New York, 1946, p.127–170.

Tall Tamare by Abraham Karpinovitch
Yiddish title: **Tamare di Hoykhe**

A former Jewish prostitute is about to be murdered by the Nazis alongside thousands of other Vilna Jews. She is inspired by her reading of a Peretz story (*Three Gifts*) to defy a German soldier's order to undress.

Pakn Treger, Spring 2009/5769, Number 59, p.38–44 (bilingual).

Bubbe Malke by Shira Gorshman
Yiddish title: **the same**

A Jewish midwife and healer, passing for a Gentile, finds work in the home of a Nazi collaborator and gathers the courage to take her vengeance.

Sandra Bark, ed., Beautiful as the Moon, Radiant as the Stars, p.279–290.
Yiddish source: Dertseylungen fun Yidishe Sovietishe Shrayber, Moscow, 1969.

Gone by Kadya Molodowsky
Yiddish title: **Oys**

A Jew living in America takes great pleasure in his regular trips to his hometown in Eastern Europe, where he dispenses gifts and stories about the good life—until the Nazis destroy the town and wipe out his family.

Molodowsky, A House with Seven Windows, p.65–69.
Yiddish source: A Shtub Mit Zibn Fentster, New York, 1957.

The Erased Sign by Tsvi Eisenman
Yiddish title: **Dos Opgemekte Shildl**

A Holocaust survivor returns to his childhood home in Poland after 50 years. The village looks the same, but the building where he lived has been replaced and the home of his murdered sweetheart is occupied by strangers. Before leaving, he washes his hands, a ritual performed upon returning from a cemetery.

Tsvi Eisenman, At the Edge of Dreamland, p. 54–58
Yiddish source: Baym Rand fun Kholem

The Wedding Dress by Tsvi Eisenman
Yiddish title: **Dos Khupe-Kleyd**

An old lame widow, a Holocaust survivor, lives unhappily in a nursing home. To cheer herself up, she sneaks out with her walker to look at the gowns in a bridal shop window. But this brings back sad memories of her own threadbare wedding to another survivor in the aftermath of the war.

Tsvi Eisenman, At the Edge of Dreamland, p. 168-170
Yiddish source: Baym Rand fun Kholem

Anti-Semitism

In the Mail Coach by I.L. Peretz (also see **Women**)
Yiddish title: **Inem Post-Vogn**

Peretz, who places himself in this story, encounters an old Polish friend who vigorously denounces anti-Semitism among his fellow Poles. Peretz questions the Pole's motives, but there appears to be no evidence to justify his suspicions. The lesson here may be that Polish anti-Semitism was so pervasive that even an enlightened Jew would see it where it did not exist.

Wisse, The I.L. Peretz Reader, p.104-118.
Yiddish source: Ale Verk—Y.L. Perets, 15: 166-172, Vilna 1925-29.

A German makes a blood accusation and is flogged near the bathhouse before the entire community by I. J. Singer
Yiddish title: **A Daytsh makht an aliles-dam un me shmayst im lebn bod far gants kol in di oygn**

In this memoir by I. B. Singer's older brother, a pogrom is averted when a Russian governor, whose palm is greased by a rich Jew, beats a German into confessing that he fabricated a ritual murder accusation. However, the governor's motive is not to protect Jewish lives. It is to preserve "order."

Of a World That is No More by I. J. Singer, p.48-54.
Yiddish source: Fun a Velt Vos Iz Nishto Mer, New York, 1946.

A Country Passover by Sholem Aleichem
Yiddish title: **Peysekh in Dorf**

The idyllic friendship between two village boys, one Jewish and the other Gentile, barely survives a ritual murder scare. Even under the best of circumstances, the Christian villagers believe that their Jewish neighbor just might kill one of their children to use his blood to bake matza.

Sholem Aleichem, The Old Country, p.336-346;
and Goldberg, Yiddish Stories for Young People, p.172-178.
Yiddish source: Oreme un Freylekhe: Tsveyter Buch, AV'42, Band 1,
Daled: 163-178.

The Malicious Matza by Sholem Aleichem
Yiddish title: Di Geferlekhe Matse

A Jew, in the form of a matza, inhabits the stomach of a king and refuses to leave until the king rescinds an anti-Semitic decree.

Sholem Aleichem, Old Country Tales, p.278-280.
Yiddish source: Lekoved Yontif, Tsveyter Bukh, AV'42, Band 1, Daled:
201-04.

Two Anti-Semites by Sholem Aleichem
Yiddish title: Tsvey Antisemitn

A self-hating Jew gets his comeuppance, but at least he can take a joke.

Howe and Wisse, The Best of Sholem Aleichem, p.144-154;
and Sholem Aleichem, Old Country Tales, p.206-213.
Yiddish source: Oreme un Freylekhe: Tsveyter Bukh, AV'42, Band 4,
Daled: 151-161.

The Krushniker Delegation by Sholem Aleichem
Yiddish title: Mayses Fun Toyznt Eyn Nakht

A serious Sholem Aleichem fictionalizes events from his lifetime— the massacres of Jews that occurred on the Russian front during WWI. (He died in 1916, before much worse massacres occurred.)

Howe and Wisse, The Best of Sholem Aleichem, p.291-307.
Yiddish source: Mayses Un Fantazyes, AV'42, Band 3, Hey: 137-232.

Acquiring a Graveyard by Abraham Reisen
Yiddish title: **Der Ervorbener Beys-oylem**

In this grim tale, set in World War I, death comes to an isolated shtetl from "friend" and foe alike.

Neugroschel, Shtetl: a creative anthology of Jewish Life in Eastern Europe, p.481-484.
Yiddish source: Ale Verk fun Avrom Reyzin, vol. 2, Amolike Mentshn, 1917.

How Long Does a Pogrom Last? by Alexander Kapel
Yiddish title: **Vifl Doyert A Pogrom?**

A shopkeeper is tormented by abusive Gentile customers and extortion by government officials. He and his wife suffer in silence, only to be totally ruined by a pogrom.

Neugroschel, No Star Too Beautiful, p.394-402.
Yiddish source: Ertseylungen un Skitsen, 1911.

Kola Street by Sholem Asch
Yiddish title: **Dos Koyler Gesl**
Led by a tough family, working class Jews—the *proste Yidn* (coarse Jews) held in contempt by their more educated and prosperous brethren—defend the entire Jewish community from attack. This is a powerful story remarkable for its graphic description of violence.

Howe and Greenberg, A Treasury of Yiddish Stories, p.260-275.
Yiddish source: Fun Shtetl tsu der Groyser Velt, Musterverk series, Buenos Aires, 1972; and Gezamlte Shriften, Himel un erd, vol. 3, Sholem Ash Komitet, 1921, p.21-44.

How the Fight Began by Joseph Opatoshu
Yiddish title: **In Kar**

On a streetcar in an American city, Jews fight back against anti-Semitic hoodlums.

Rosenfeld, Pushcarts and Dreamers, p.137-140.
Yiddish source: Gezamlte Verk, vol. 5, Lintsheray un andere
dertseylungen, Kletskin, Vilna, 1927; and Rase, Lintsheray un andere
dertseylungen, Peretz-bibliotek, Warsaw, 1923.

Little Souls by Leon Kobrin
Yiddish title: **Kleyne Neshomelekh**

A Jewish worker who sticks up for a fellow worker abused by an anti-Semitic foreman is shocked to learn that his help was not welcome.

Rosenfeld, Pushcarts and Dreamers, p.53-63.
Yiddish source: Gezamlte Shriften, Hebrew Publishing Company, 1910,
p.696-707.

Hannukah in the Poor House by Isaac Bashevis Singer
(See **Holiday Stories**)

For a Better World

If I Were Rothschild by Sholem Aleichem
Yiddish title: **Ven Ikh Bin Roytshild**

A poor Jewish school teacher muses on how he would cure the ills of the world if he had Rothschild's fortune, but is brought back to reality by the thought that he does not have enough money to prepare for Shabes. This story, although it does not feature the Tevye character, is the basis for the song "If I Were A Rich Man" from the play and movie Fiddler on the Roof.

*Howe and Wisse, The Best of Sholem Aleichem, p.162-166; and
Sholem Aleichem, Tevye's Daughters, p. 16-19
Yiddish source: Kleyne Mentshelekh Mit Kleyne Hasoges, AV'42, Band
5, Beys: 129-133.*

May God Have Mercy by Sholem Aleichem
Yiddish title: **Nisht Far Keyn Yidn Gedakht**

When a rich man's son takes over his father's money-lending business and proceeds to forgive all of the townspeople's debts, they refuse to accept their good fortune. They complain to the rabbi, who tries to convince the man that money-lending is a legitimate business. The man responds by not only repudiating money-lending, but also denouncing social injustice and the barbarism of modern warfare. Unable to envision alternatives to the society he lives in, the rabbi concludes that the rich man's son is a lunatic. The townspeople agree.

*Sholem Aleichem, Tevye's Daughters, p.141-144.
Yiddish source: Kleyne Mentshelekh Mit Kleyne Hasoges, AV'42, Band
5, Beys: 53-58.*

Pity for Living Things by Sholem Aleichem
Yiddish title: **Tsar Baley-Khayim**

A boy is taught by his rabbi that God wishes people to show compassion for all living things. However, so much of what the boy sees in real life—the slaughter of animals, cruelty to pets and the murder of his neighbor's disabled daughter in a pogrom—contradicts this principle. Yet the boy holds fast to his belief.

*Shevrin, A Treasury of Sholem Aleichem's Children's Stories, p.173-179.
Yiddish source: Mayses far Yidishe Kinder: Ershter Bukh, Band 1, Hey:
193-200.*

Dreyfus in Kasrilevke by Sholem Aleichem
Yiddish title: **same**

Shtetl Jews take an intense interest in the fate of Dreyfus. Convinced of his innocence, they refuse to accept the news of his second conviction, blaming instead the messenger—a Jew who read the report from the newspaper. (Dreyfus was, of course, later vindicated.)

Howe and Wisse, The Best of Sholem Aleichem, p 139-143; and Howe and Greenberg, A Treasury of Yiddish Stories, p.187-192.
Yiddish source: Kleyne Mentshelekh Mit Kleyne Hasoges, AV'42 Band 5 Beys: 61-68.

Josep on the Jewish Street by Abraham Reisen
Yiddish title: **Yosep in Der Yidisher Gas**

A touching portrait of an uneducated Gentile who worked for his Jewish neighbors with love and respect.

Avrom Reisen, Poor Matza, p. 149-159
Yiddish source: Dertseylungen, Congress for Secular Jewish Culture (Tsiko), NY, 1952, p. 163.

Two Shrines by Zalman Libin
Yiddish title: **Tsvey Reynigkaytn**

A pious father, who lives with his revolutionary daughter in America, despises her politics until he learns that his son in Russia, also a revolutionary, died defending the Jewish community from a pogrom. He then treats his daughter's red flag with the same reverence as his Torah scroll.

Albert Waldinger: An Anthology of Early Yiddish Stories from the Lower East Side, p.74-77.
Yiddish source: Gezamlte Verk, vol. 1, Forverts, New York, 1915, p.145-150.

Becoming Revolutionary by Bryna Bercovitch
Yiddish title: none

In this memoir, a middle-aged woman reminisces about her life as a communist revolutionary in Russia and Canada—her early enthusiasm and her "catastrophic disillusion."

Tregebov, Arguing with the Storm: Stories by Yiddish Women Writers, p.62-76.
Yiddish source: the newspaper Der Keneder Odler, various weekly columns, 1945, '48,49,50.

Moral Choices

The Sanctification of the Name by Sholem Asch
Yiddish title: **Kidesh Ha-shem**

Five Jews are unjustly imprisoned and tortured by the authorities, but are promised their freedom and great rewards if they convert to Christianity. Four of them are respected community leaders; the fifth, a coarse workingman. He has been lax in observing the religious laws and once even threatened to convert if the town's rabbi continued to reprimand him. Will he succumb?

Howe and Greenberg, A Treasury of Yiddish Stories, p.255-260.
Yiddish source: Gezamelte Shriften, Bilder un Humoresken, Tsveyter Band, Tsveyter Oysgabe, Sholem Asch Committee, 1923.

Tuition for the Rebbe by Abraham Reisen
Yiddish title: **Skhar-limed**

A father must decide whether to cheat in business in order to earn the money to pay for his son's education. To make matters worse, he needs his son's help to pull off the deception.

Howe and Greenberg, A Treasury of Yiddish Stories, p.284-290.
Yiddish source: Ale Verk fun Avrom Reyzin, vol. 3, Heymishe
Mentchen.

A Common Language by Leon Kobrin
Yiddish title: **Di Shprakh fun Elnt**

A Jewish night watchman catches a poor Italian man stealing from his employer's property. The stolen item is nothing more than wood that the Italian needs to heat his home. The Jew lets him go, even at the cost of his job. Despite their language barrier, the two men understand each other. They are both poor immigrants struggling to survive in America.

Rosenfeld, Pushcarts and Dreamers p.29-46.
Yiddish source: Der Farloyrener Nign: roman un zeks dertseylugen,
IKUF Farlag, New York, 1948, p.245-261.

The Washwoman by Isaac Bashevis Singer
Yiddish title: **Di Veshin**

In this memoir of his boyhood, Isaac recalls with reverence a poor old Gentile washerwoman, disowned by her wealthy son, who survives a near fatal illness in order to return his family's laundry before dying.

Isaac Bashevis Singer, In My Father's Court, p.29-33.
Yiddish source: Mayn Tatn's Bezdn Shtub, 1954.

Hard Luck by Sholem Aleichem
Yiddish title: **Nito Kayn Mazl!**

In this story about an "honest" thief and his victim, a businessman, the two translations provide different versions of the businessman's reaction to the culprit's arrest! The one in which the businessman expresses remorse about reporting the crime appears to be the accurate one.

Sholem Aleichem, Tevye the Dairyman and the Railroad Stories, p.255-259; and Old Country Tales (No Luck), p.174-178.
Yiddish source: Ayznban Geshikhtes: Ksovim Fun a Komivoyazher, AV'42, Band 5, Hey: 245-251.

The Miracle of Hoshana Rabbah by Sholem Aleichem
Yiddish title: Der Nes Fun Heshayne-Rabe

An audacious Jew and a Russian priest debate the meaning of life and death while courting disaster aboard a runaway train.

Sholem Aleichem, Tevye the Dairyman and the Railroad Stories, p.186-194; and The Old Country, p.228-238.
Yiddish source: Ayznban Geshikhtes: Ksovim Fun a Komivoyazher, AV'42, Band 5, Hey: 113-126.

Go Talk to a Goy! by S. Ansky
Yiddish title: A Goyisher Kop

A Gentile woman involved in the Russian revolutionary movement is summoned by her party to move to a big city. She cannot do so under her own name because of her police record, so she adopts a false Jewish identity. But Jews cannot live there without special permission or bribing police officials. A Jewish party comrade has a brilliant idea. Let her pretend to convert to Christianity. This will get the police off her back, so she can pursue her revolutionary work. But the Gentile woman refuses to go along with the ruse out of respect for those who are sincerely religious. The Jewish party comrade is flabbergasted at this display of "bourgeois morality."

S. Ansky, The Dybbuk and Other Writings, p.145-150.
Yiddish source: Noveln, Gezamlte Shriftn, NY, 1920-1925, vol. 1, p.127-135.

Alter Iteleh's and His Daughters by Kadya Molodowsky
Yiddish title: Alter Iteleh's Un Zayne Tekhter

A rich man whose doors are always open to his fellow Jews and who, along with his daughters, serves the community in many ways, has to make a difficult decision when his pretentious wife proposes to install a new shiny floor in their home to keep out the riff-raff.

Molodowsky, A House with Seven Windows, p.269-273.
Yiddish source: A Shtub Mit Zibn Fentster, New York, 1957.

Heroes by Jacob Gordin
Yiddish title: **Heldn**

A group of American Jewish intellectuals discusses the case of an American Indian who killed a vicious U.S. government official and turned himself in after converting to Christianity.

Goodman, The New Country, p.421-425.
Yiddish source: Ale Shriftn fun Yaakov Gordin, vol.1, Hebrew Publishing Company, New York, p.174-178.

Spirituality

If Not Higher by I.L. Peretz
Yiddish title: **Oyb Nit Nokh Hekher**

In this famous tale, a skeptical Lithuanian Jew (a Litvak) tracks a Hasidic *rebbe* to disprove the popular notion that he ascends to Heaven just before Yom Kippur. What he discovers, however, is more awe-inspiring. The *rebbe*, disguised as a peasant, helps a poor sick Jewish woman heat her home. The Litvak then becomes one of the *rebbe*'s disciples.

Katz, Y.L. Peretz, Selected Stories—Bilingual Edition (Geklibene Dertseylungen), p.270-281; Wisse, The I.L. Peretz Reader, p.178-181; Howe and Greenberg, A Treasury of Yiddish Stories, p.231-233; and Weinstein, Prophets & Dreamers, p.43-46.

Between Two Mountains by I.L. Peretz
Yiddish title: **Tvishn Tsvey Berg**
The Hasidic belief that Judaism should be an egalitarian creed that speaks to the heart of the ordinary Jew is contrasted with the arid and oppressive legalism of the rabbinic establishment, i.e the *misnagdim*

Wisse, The I.L. Peretz Reader, p.184-195.
Yiddish source: "Tsvishn tsvey berg" in Khsidish, Volume 4, Ale verk—Y.L. Perets, Volume 4, New York: Farlag "Idish," 1920.

The Musician's Death by I.L. Peretz
Yiddish title: **A Klezmer-toyt**

Here Peretz offers a different view of spirituality; one expressed by a dying musician who insists that his sons play at his death bed rather than pray.

Wisse, The I.L. Peretz Reader, p.125-127.
Yiddish source: Ertseylungen, Mayselekh, Poemen un proza, Ale Verk—Y.L. Perets, vol. 8, New York: Farlag "Idish," 1920.

"Our" First of May by David Pinski
Yiddish title: **'Undzer' Ershter May**

A Jewish immigrant in America reminisces about the heroism and idealism of Jewish revolutionaries in Czarist Russia who celebrated May Day despite the ever-present threat of police repression.

Waldinger, Shining and Shadow: An Anthology of Early Yiddish Stories from the Lower East Side, p.129-131.
Yiddish source: Ertseylungen, International Library Publishing, 1906-1907, p.280-284.

At a Picnic by Miriam Raskin
Yiddish title: **Oyf A Piknik**

A middle aged Jewish woman finds inspiration and camaraderie within the American socialist movement.

Forman et al., Found Treasures-Stories by Yiddish Women Writers, p.203-209.
Yiddish source: Shtile Lebns, Group of Friends, New York, 1941.

Education

Gy-Ma-Na-Si-A by Sholem Aleichem
Yiddish title: **Gimenazya**

A Jewish mother moves heaven and earth to overcome anti-Jewish quotas. After many ordeals, she gains admission for her son to a Russian high school. But her success is short lived. The boy joins a student strike and quits the school in protest.

Sholem Aleichem, Tevye's Daughters, p. 225-238
Yiddish source: Ayzenban Geshikhtes, AV'42, Band 5, Hey 175

A Useless Man by Abraham Reisen
Yiddish title: **An Iberiker Mentsh**

A boorish landlord ridicules an eccentric intellectual who is helping his son with his doctoral dissertation.

Abraham Reisen, Poor Matza, p. 24-26
Yiddish source: Lider, Derteylungen, Zikhroynes, YIVO, Buenos Aires, 1966, p. 247-249

Gershon by Chaver Paver (an excerpt from a novel)
Yiddish title: none

New Jewish immigrants to America, exhausted from their hard

day's work, flock to night school to learn English and expand their horizons.

Rosenfeld, Pushcarts and Dreamers, p.213-214.
Yiddish source: Gershn in Amerike, Farlag Yiddish Bukh, Warsaw (1963).

Parents and Children

The Joys of Parenthood by Sholem Aleichem
Yiddish title: **Nakhes Fun Kinder**

In this wry commentary on Jewish "family values" in the shtetl, a proud father brags about his children and their spouses, except for two of them: one, a son-in-law, a plain workingman who happens to be the only one who is self-supporting; the other, a loyal daughter-in-law whom he disparages—until she starts having children.

Sholem Aleichem, Tevye's Daughters, p.109-113.
Yiddish source: Kleyne Mentshelekh Mit Kleyne Hasoges, AV' 42, Band 5, Beys: 33-40.

The Inheritors by Sholem Aleichem
Yiddish title: **Di Yorshim**

In this tragic-comic tale of sibling rivalry, two sons disgrace themselves by fighting over their father's legacy—a prime seat in *shul* by the Eastern wall.

Sholem Aleichem, The Old Country, p.8-20.
Yiddish source: Kleyne Mentshelekh Mit Kleyne Hasoges, AV'42, Band 5, Beys: 137-154.

Shut In by Abraham Reisen
Yiddish title: **Farmakht**

A strict religious upbringing stifles a boy's natural love of the outdoors and his desire to play.

Schwarz, Leo, ed., The Jewish Caravan, p.315-317; and Abraham Reisen, The Heart-Stirring Sermon and Other Stories, p.79-82.
Yiddish source: Ale Verk fun Avrom Reyzin, vol. 8, Oreme Gemeynden.

To the New World by Isaac Metzker
Yiddish title: **none**

A traditional Jewish family in Eastern Europe can't control their rebellious son. So they send him to America. He is the first one in his village to make the move, but he certainly won't be the last.

Howe and Greenberg, A Treasury of Yiddish Stories, p 504-515.
Yiddish source: condensed and adapted from his novel, Oyfn Zeyden's Felder (Grandfather's Acres), 1953.

Generations by Peretz Markish (excerpt from a novel)
Yiddish title: none

Modern times, in the form of Darwinism, revolutionary politics and industrialization, create tensions between father and son in Czarist Russia.

Neugroschel, The Shtetl: a creative anthology of Jewish life in Eastern Europe, p.459-470.
Yiddish source: Dor Oys, Dor Ayn, kapitl 1, Warsaw, 1964.

Solomon by Isaac Raboy
Yiddish title: **the same**

In America, a daughter rebels against her rich father by denouncing him in the Yiddish press as a capitalist exploiter and taking a job in his factory as an ordinary worker.

Schwarz, ed., The Jewish Caravan, p.606-613.
Yiddish source: Ikh Dertsehl, Farlage Amerike, New York, 1920, p.165-177.

The Son by Isaac Bashevis Singer
Yiddish title: **Der Zun**

A father in America is re-united with a son from Israel, whom he has not seen for twenty years. In the interim, Jews died under Hitler, suffered under Stalin and fought for their own state. Will they be able to emotionally connect after all that has transpired in their separate lives and in the Jewish world?

Jerry D. Lewis, ed., Tales of Our People, p.325-332; and Isaac Bashevis Singer Collected Stories: A Friend of Kafka to Passions, p.208-214.
Yiddish source: Gimpl Tam un Andere Dertseylungen, CYCO, 1963.

The Lost Shabes by Kadya Molodowsky
Yiddish title: **Der Farlorener Shabes**

A little American Jewish girl savors the bit of Yiddishkayt she gets from her Yiddish speaking grandfather and elderly neighbor, because she does not get enough of it from her semi-assimilated mother.

Melanie Kaye/Kantrowitz and Irena Klepfisz, eds., The Tribe of Dina—A Jewish Women's Anthology, p.146-147; and Molodowsky, A House with Seven Windows, p.198-200.
Yiddish source: A Shtub Mit Zibn Fentster, New York, 1957.

On Saint Katerine's Day by Lili Berger
Yiddish title: **In Tog Fun Der Heyliker Katerina**

A daughter of Holocaust victims, raised as a Catholic in Poland, discovers her Jewish past. She loves her adoptive parents, but seeks to reconnect with any surviving Jewish relatives.

Forman et al., Found Treasures-Stories by Yiddish Women Writers, p.223-235.
Yiddish source: Fun Haynt un Nekhtn, Wydawnictwo Idisz Buch, Warsaw, 1965.

The Four-Ruble War by Helen Londynski
Yiddish title: **Fir-Rubldike Milkhome**

In this memoir, a young Jewish woman from a devout Chasidic family must choose between continuing her secular education and maintaining her father's love.

Bark, ed., Beautiful as the Moon, Radiant as the Stars, p.83-100.
Yiddish source: In Shpigl fun Nekhtn: Zikhroyes, NY, 1972, p.11-20.

A Guest by Sarah Hamer-Jacklyn
Yiddish title: A **Gast**

An immigrant mother living with her Canadian-born son and daughter-in-law is gradually excluded from all contact with her grandson over differences on their approaches toward child-rearing. Rather than suffer humiliation, the mother gets a job, moves out and becomes an independent woman.

Tregebov, Arguing with the Storm: Stories by Yiddish Women Writers, p.33-49.
Yiddish source: Lebns un Geshtaltn: Dertseylungen, The Novoradomsker Society, New York, 1946.

The Plight of Women

A Lesson in Morality by I.L. Peretz
Yiddish title: **Musar**

A poor widow, who bitterly regrets that she raised her two older daughters according to strict Jewish law, lets her youngest daughter taste freedom.

Katz, Selected Stories of Y.L. Peretz—Bilingual Edition (Geklibene Dertseylungen), p.102-116.

In the Mail Coach by I.L. Peretz
Yiddish title: **Inem Post-Vogn** (also see **Anti-Semitism**)

The shtetl environment sucks the life out of Jewish women not content with their traditional lot as wife and mother.

Wisse, The I.L. Peretz Reader, p.104-118.
Yiddish source: Ale Verk—Y.L. Perets, 15: 166-172, Vilna 1925-29.

My Mother's Dream by Sarah Hamer-Jacklyn
Yiddish title: **Mayn Mame's Kholem**

In a traditional Jewish home in Eastern Europe, prejudices and superstitions operate to devalue the humanity of a young girl.

Forman et al., Found Treasures-Stories by Yiddish Women Writers, p.65-76.
Yiddish source: Shtamen un Tsvayg, Novoradomsker Society, NY, 1954.

Equality of the Sexes by Abraham Reisen
Yiddish title: **Glaykhkayt**

When a Jewish woman in America starts earning as much as her fiancée and insists on paying for dinner, the man is forced to re-think his notions of male supremacy.

Rosenfeld, New Yorkish and Other American Yiddish Stories, p.160-166.
Yiddish source: Gezamlte Shriftn, vol. 9, 1916.

Apartment No. Four by Leon Kobrin
Yiddish title: **Tir num. 4**

An abused Jewish prostitute in New York's Lower East Side takes vengeance on her attacker, a co-owner of the brothel, and denounces his female partner (both Jews) to her neighbors.

Neugroschel, No Star Too Beautiful, p.534-540.
Yiddish source: Fun a Litvish Shtetl biz'n Tenement Hoyz, Forverts, New York, 1918, p.340-350.

Rosh Hashanah by Yente Serdatsky
Yiddish title: **Rosh Hashana**

In this tale of loneliness and alienation, a young Jewish woman in America, exiled from Russia for her revolutionary activities, misses her imprisoned comrades. However, when Rosh Hashana arrives, she misses the spirit of the holiday and her saintly grandfather even more.

Bark, ed., Beautiful as the Moon, Radiant as the Stars, p. 233-241.
Yiddish source: Geklibene Shriftn (1913).

Marriage

Happiness in Marriage by I.L. Peretz
Yiddish title: **Sholem Bayis**

A poor couple's love endures despite their hard life. The husband, a simple illiterate worker, admires the learned Jews, but when his rabbi tells him that his wife will be his "footstool" in Paradise, he insists that she will sit beside him as an equal.

Katz, Y.L. Peretz Selected Stories—Bilingual Edition (Geklibene Dertseylungen), p.2-10.

Uncle Shakhne and Aunt Yakhne by I.L. Peretz
Yiddish title: **Der Feter Shakhne un di Mume Yakhne**

The story of two marriages, one successful and the other a failure, are intertwined with humor and pathos.

Wisse, The I.L. Peretz Reader, p. 171-178.
Yiddish source: Ertseylungen, Ale Verk—Y.L. Perets, vol. 3, New York: Farlag "Idish," 1920.

A White Bird by Sholem Aleichem
Yiddish title: **Vayse Kapore**

A modern woman's obsession with performing the *kapores* atonement ceremony on Yom Kippur, involving the sacrifice of a bird, appears to be a peculiar reaction to her failed marriage.

Sholem Aleichem, Old Country Tales, p.161-167.
Yiddish source: Monologn, Ale Verk Fun Sholem Aleichem, Folksfond Oysgabe, New York: Folksfond, 1917-1923, XXI: 47-54, 1921.

The Son-in-Law by Kadya Molodowsky
Yiddish title: **Der Eydem**

A mother who lives to please her "son-in-law the doctor" endures his insults. When her daughter complains of similar treatment, the mother insists that she submit to him.
Molodowsky, A House with Seven Windows, p.58-64.
Yiddish source: A Shtub Mit Zibn Fentster, New York, 1957.

Intermarriage

Chava by Sholem Aleichem
Yiddish title: **Chava**

Get Thee Out by Sholem Aleichem
Yiddish title: **Lekh-Lekho**

In these two excerpts, Tevye grapples with his daughter's marriage to a Gentile. As a product of his environment, Tevye can only conclude that she has committed a terrible sin and accordingly, he pronounces her dead. But there are doubts clouding his outrage, and the possibility is left open at the end that his love for her will prevail.

Howe and Wisse, The Best of Sholem Aleichem, p.222-225, 240-243; and Sholem Aleichem, Tevye's Daughters, p.93-108, 257-272.
Yiddish source for Chava: Tevye Der Milkhiker, AV'42, Band 5, Giml: 121-140 and for Lekh-Lekho: Tevye Der Milkhiker, AV'42, Band 5, Giml: 199-220.

Mabel's Secret by Shimshon Apter
Yiddish title: **Maybls Sod**

A Jewish woman is ostracized from her family because of her romance and marriage to a Black man. Although happily married, when she falls ill, she yearns to be reunited with them.

Rosenfeld, New Yorkish and Other American Jewish Stories, p.201-213.
Yiddish source: the journal Zukunft, July-August 1976.

Her Story by Chava Slucka-Kestin
Yiddish title: **Ir Geshikhte**

A Jewish woman who survived the Holocaust immigrates to Israel. She marries and has a son with a Jewish man who neglects her. She falls in love with an Arab, gets a divorce and remarries. She loses her son to her vindictive ex-husband, but has more children with her new husband and finds acceptance in the Arab community. Still the old wounds remain.

Forman et al., Found Treasures–Stories by Yiddish Women Writers, p.317-328
Yiddish source: In Undzere Teg, Farlag Meyer, Tel Aviv, 1966.

HOLIDAY STORIES

Rosh Hashana

If Not Higher by I.L. Peretz   (See **Spirituality**)

Rosh Hashanah by Yente Serdatsky   (See **The Plight of Women**)

Yom Kippur

Yom Kippur in Hell by I.L. Peretz
Yiddish title: **Nile in Gehenem**

A cantor with a golden voice is solely responsible for keeping all the dead people from his town out of Hell, until Satan contrives to rob him of his voice. In desperation, the cantor commits suicide by jumping in a river. This way his voice will remain trapped in his body. As a suicide, he is condemned to Hell, but he unleashes his voice there and sings so beautifully that all of Hell's inmates join in and escape to Heaven. The cantor alone remains, but not for long. There is a plentiful supply of new arrivals.

Wisse, The I.L. Peretz Reader, p.258-262; and Howe and Greenberg, A Treasury of Yiddish Stories (Ne'ilah in Gehenna), p.213-219. Yiddish source: Ale Verk—Y.L. Perets, 15:166-172, Vilna 1925-29.

The Day Before Yom Kippur by Sholem Aleichem
Yiddish title: **Men iz Zikh Moykhl**

A touching evocation of the custom requiring all Jews to ask forgiveness from those they have wronged in the previous year. But the suspicion lingers that these apologies may be mere formalities.

Sholem Aleichem, The Old Country, p.319-328.
Yiddish source: Oreme Un Freylekhe: Tsveyter Bukh, AV'42 Band 4, Daled: 193-223.

A Yom Kippur Scandal by Sholem Aleichem
Yiddish title: **Oysgetreyslt**

A theft of money occurs in *shul* during the Yom Kippur service. In order to find the culprit, the rabbi orders that all congregants be searched. Only one man refuses. He is the son-in-law of one of the town's leading citizens, with a reputation as a scholar. But it is not because he is the thief. Rather it is because he has eaten on this most solemn of fast days. When he is taken by force and the search turns up evidence of food in his pockets, that exposure becomes the greater scandal.

Howe and Wisse, The Best of Sholem Aleichem, p.47-53; Howe and Greenberg, A Treasury of Yiddish Stories (The Search), p.182-187; and Weinstein, Prophets & Dreamers, p.77-82.
Yiddish source: Kleyne Menshtelekh Mit Kleyne Hasoges, AV'42 Band 5, Beys: 213-221.

Sukkos

Too Late by Abraham Reisen
Yiddish title: **Farshpetikt**

A Gentile peasant, whose livelihood depends on selling wood to Jews for the building of their *Sukkos*, arrives in town after the holiday has begun. The Jewish townspeople have compassion for him, and although forbidden to carry money on a holiday, they give him the household goods he needs to survive. The second adult version has more of an edge, as the Jews initially ridicule the peasant and, at the very end, allude to their fear of Gentile violence.

Goldberg, Yiddish Stories For Young People, p.72-77; and Reisen, The Heart-Stirring Sermon and Other Stories, p.127-134.
Yiddish source: Dertseylungen, Central Yiddish Cultural Organization (Tsiko), New York, 1952, p.139-146.

The Big Succah by Abraham Reisen
Yiddish title: **Di Groyse Suke**

A poor Jew can't fit his relatives into his tiny home, so he makes up for it on *Sukkos* by building the biggest *suke* in the neighborhood.

Howe and Greenberg, A Treasury of Yiddish Stories, p.280-284.
Yiddish source: Ale Verk fun Avrom Reyzin, vol. 3, Heymishe Mentshn.

Simkhes Toyre

The Flag by Sholem Aleichem
Yiddish title: **Di Fon**

A poor boy, teased because of a speech defect, comes into good fortune, resists temptation and spends it on a handsome *Simkhes Toyre* flag, complete with apple and candle. A rich jealous boy maliciously has it set on fire. Our hero is devastated, but just wait till next year...

from Sholem Aleichem, Old Country Tales, p.73-84; and Goldberg, Yiddish Stories For Young People (The Simchas Torah Flag), p.78-85.
Yiddish source: Mayses far Yiddishe Kinder: Tsveyter Bukh, AV'42 Band 1, Vov.

David, King Of Israel by Sholem Aleichem
Yiddish title: **Dovid Meylekh Yisroel**

During the rest of the year, an ancient Jew collects food and clothing for Jewish prisoners. On *Simkhes Toyre*, he leads the children in a merry parade—until a vindictive police chief locks him up.

Sholem Aleichem, Old Country Tales, p.272-277; and Shevrin, A Treasury of Sholom Aleichem Children's Stories, p.269-277.
Yiddish source: Fun Peysekh Biz Peysekh, AV'42 Band 5, Alef: 175-183.

The Merrymakers by Sholem Aleichem
(See **Life in the Shtetl**)

Khanike

Chanukah Money by Sholem Aleichem
Yiddish title: **Khanike Gelt**

Two brothers make the rounds of their relatives, each with their own idiosyncrasies, collecting *Khanike gelt* (money). The boys are thrilled with their haul, but can't manage to figure out the total amount they collected.

Sholem Aleichem, The Old Country, p.183-199.
Yiddish source: Mayses Far Yiddishe Kinder: Tsveyter Bukh, AV'42 Band 1, Vov: 29-50.

Cnards by Sholem Aleichem   Yiddish title: **Knortn**

A gang of fanatical card players gets together on Khanike, the only period when it is permitted to gamble. Their card-playing is interrupted by mysterious visitors—the *Baal Shem Tov's* (the founder of the Hasidic movement) grandson and his assistant, collecting contributions for yeshivas throughout the world. The card players seize the opportunity to swindle them out of their money, but wait and see who has the last laugh.

Sholem Aleichem, The Old Country, p.372-388.
Yiddish source: Lekoved Yontif: Ershter Bukh, AV'42 Band 1 Giml: 201-222.

The Parakeet Named Dreidel by Isaac Bashevis Singer
Yiddish title: unknown

A Yiddish-speaking parakeet, rescued from the cold of winter, brings two families together on Khanike.

Isaac Bashevis Singer, Stories for Children, p.98-102.
Yiddish source: not published in book form.

Hannukah in the Poorhouse by Isaac Bashevis Singer
Yiddish title: unknown

An old traveler sitting among paupers, tells how he was drafted into the Russian Army as a boy and forced to adopt Christian practices. Nevertheless, he prayed and lit Khanike candles in secret to keep his Judaism alive. After many privations, he escaped and returns to his shtetl, only to discover that his betrothed died of disease. Lighting Khanike candles, whether it is Khanike or not, is all he has left to lift his spirits.

Isaac Bashevis Singer, Stories for Children, p.271-282.
Yiddish source: not published in book form.

Purim

Visiting With King Ahasuerus by Sholem Aleichem
Yiddish title: **Baym Kenig Akhashveres**

A rich man's son sneaks out of his home to celebrate Purim with a band of poor *Purim-shpielers* (performers). Class hatreds boil to the surface when his snobbish father and his hated tutor burst in to ruin his fun.

Sholem Aleichem, Old Country Tales, p.51-64; and Shevrin, A Treasury of Sholom Aleichem Children's Stories, p.19-35.
Yiddish source: Mayses far Yiddishe Kinder: TsveyterBukh, AV'42 Band 1,Vov: 53-71.

The Purim Feast by Sholem Aleichem
Yiddish title: **Tsu Der Sude**

The festive spirit of the holiday is lost at a Purim banquet held at the home of a rich relation everyone fears.

Sholem Aleichem, Tevye's Daughters, p.239-246.
Yiddish source: Lekoved Yontif: Tsveyter Bukh, AV'42 Band 1, Daled: 91-102.

Purim Sweet Platters by Sholem Aleichem
Yiddish title: **Shalakhmones; A Bild**

A brief, but touching description of the custom of sending *shalakhmones.*

Sholem Aleichem, Old Country Tales, p.269-271.
Yiddish source: Lekoved Yontif, Tsveyter Bukh, AV'42 Band 1, Daled: 195-98.

Two Dead Men by Sholem Aleichem
Yiddish title: **Tsvey Toyte**

On Purim, it is "fitting and proper for a Jew to act the drunkard and a storyteller to play the fool." In this delightful tale, a drunkard and a beggar meet in a mud pile and stumble to the former's home for a Purim meal.

Sholem Aleichem, The Old Country, p.51-66.
Yiddish source: Alt-Nay Kasrilevke, AV'42 Band 4, Beys: 181-199.

Two Shalakhmones or a Purim Scandal by Sholem Aleichem
(See **Life in the Shtetl**)

Peysakh

The Magician by I.L. Peretz
Yiddish title: **Der Kuntsn-makher**

A mysterious guest provides a seder for a destitute couple too proud to ask for charity.

Wisse, The I.L. Peretz Reader, p.218-222; and Goldberg, Yiddish Stories For Young People p.179-187.
Yiddish source: Folkstimlekhe Geshikten, Ale Verk—Y.L. Perets, vol. 7, New York: Farlag "Idish," 1920.

Home for Passover by Sholem Aleichem
Yiddish title: **Oyf Pesekh Aheym**

The trials and tribulations of a school teacher trying to reach home in time for *Peysakh*. A swollen river stands in his way, but he makes it by the skin of his teeth with the help of two Gentiles—a coachman and a ferryman.

Sholem Aleichem, The Old Country, p.75-92.
Yiddish source: Lekoved Yontif, Ershter Bukh, AV'42 Band 1, Giml: 35-57.

The First Commune by Sholem Aleichem (an excerpt)
Yiddish title: **Di Ershte Komun**

Three families pool their resources to make a seder. The experiment goes smoothly, until children's laughter during the ceremony ignites a nasty feud.

Shevrin, Holiday Tales of Sholom Aleichem, p.127-141.
Yiddish source: Mayses Far Yiddishe Kinder: Tsveyter Bukh, AV'42 Band 1, Vov: 153-174.

The Passover Expropriation by Sholem Aleichem
Yiddish title: **Di Peysekhdike Ekspropriatsye**

Unemployed Jewish workers, inspired by radical ideas, invade a rich man's home and help themselves to his family's *Pesakh* seder.

Howe and Wisse, The Best of Sholem Aleichem, p.153-161; and Sholem Aleichem, Tevye's Daughters, p.273-280.
Yiddish source: Alt-Nay Kasrilevke, AV'42 Band 4, Beys: 143-153.

Shevuos

Three Little Heads by Sholem Aleichem
(See **The Curse of Poverty**)

Lag Boymer

Bandits by Sholem Aleichem (See **Life in the Shtetl**)

Shabbes

The Sabbath of the Poor by Mendele Mokher-Sforim
(excerpt from a novel)
Yiddish title: none

The joy and peace of a traditional shabbes afford a poor Jew the
only opportunity to feel like a human being.

*Edmond Fleg, The Jewish Anthology, p.331-332; and S.Y. Abramovitsch,
The Wishing Ring: A Novel, p.78-79.*
*Yiddish source: Mendele Mokher Sforim, Geklibene Verk, Dos
Vintshfingerl, Bukh 3, Kapitl 2,Band 4, New York: Ikuf, 1946-1949.*

The Lost Shabes by Kadya Molodovsky
(See **Parents and Children**)

A Union for Shabbos by Sholem Asch
(See **When Workers Organize**)

AUTHORS

S. Ansky (b. 1863 White Russia, d. 1920 Poland), pen name of Solomon Rappaport

Ansky is best known for the play *The Dybbuk,* which appeared in Yiddish in 1919 as *Tvishn Tsvey Veltn (Between Two Worlds)—Der Dibuk.* Based on Jewish folklore, it tells the story of a young married Hasidic woman possessed by the spirit of the man she was intended to marry, whose love is so powerful that even an exorcism cannot remove it. First written in Russian and then in Yiddish, it has since been translated into numerous languages and performed all over the world.

Ansky was a remarkable combination of intellectual and activist. In various stages of his life, he worked as a coal miner among gentiles, a bookbinder among Jews and served as the personal secretary to a radical Russian political philosopher and organized expeditions to collect Jewish artifacts and folklore throughout Eastern Europe. During World War I used his Russian military rank to travel through out the war zone providing relief and rescue for the beleaguered Jewish communities, delivering food and medicine and preventing looting, violence and expulsions. He wrote about this experience in *Der Yidisher Khurbn (The Jewish Catastrophe)* available in English as *The Enemy at His Pleasure* (2002).

Like so many other Jews of his generation, he received a traditional Jewish education but was won over by the ideas of the *Haskalah* and later joined the Russian revolutionary movement against the czar. From 1892 to 1905, he lived as a political exile in France. After the failed 1905 revolution, he took a greater interest in Jewish affairs and began writing in Yiddish—poetry, novels, short stories and plays. Many explored the generational and ideological clash between tradition and modernity.

He participated in the 1917 revolution against the czar and was elected to the Constituent Assembly, in the first free election in Russian history. After the Bolsheviks disbanded it in January 1918, he fled to Poland to escape arrest and died there two years later.

A single collection of his stories exists in English translation, edited by David Roskies. Two are referenced here, one a memoir of his ill-fated youthful attempt to "enlighten" a *shtetl* which also appears in Lucy Davidowicz's classic anthology *The Golden Tradition*.

Shimshon Apter (b. 1907 Poland, d. 1986, New York)

A novelist, short story writer and historian, Apter began his literary career in Warsaw. In 1930, he immigrated to Canada and wrote for the Toronto Yiddish press. In 1936, he moved to New York where he attended the Jewish Teachers Seminary.

Apter wrote short story collections, historical novels as well as a book of medieval Jewish history. His novel, *The Preisingers* (1980) has been translated into English.

The story referenced here is unusual for its subject matter—interracial marriage.

Sholem Asch (b. Poland 1880, d. England 1957)

Before Isaac Bashevis Singer outraged refined Jewish sensibilities, Asch was the most controversial—and popular—figure in Yiddish literature for his depictions of raw emotions, violence and sex. He also provoked a huge outcry by his favorable portrayals of Jesus, Mary and early Christianity.

Like many other Yiddish writers, Asch began writing in Hebrew, but under the influence of Peretz, turned to Yiddish to reach a popular audience. He first came to the U.S. in 1910, but returned to Poland after World War I and then lived in France before retuning to the U.S. in 1938.

Primarily a novelist and a playwright, his work explored diverse themes of Jewish criminality, heroism and martyrdom. He broke new ground with his play *Der Got fun Nekome* (*God of Vengeance)* (1913) which dealt with prostitution and lesbianism and his novel *Motke der Ganev* (1917), concerning Jewish thieves.

He also wrote novels of social realism including *Onkl Mozes*

(*Uncle Moses*) (1918) and *Ist River (East River)* (1946), about Jewish immigrant life in the U.S. and the trilogy, *Farn Mabl: Moskve, Petersberg, Varshe (Before the Flood: Moscow, St. Petersburg, Warsaw) (1930-37)*, translated in one volume as *Three Cities*, dealing with Jewish life amid social upheavals in urban Russia and Poland.

During and after World War II, Asch published three novels, *Der Man fun Notseres* (*The Nazarene*), *Meri* (*Mary*) and *Der Apostol* also known as *Der Sheliekh* (*The Apostle*), where he attempted to reclaim Jesus and early Christianity as a Jewish movement worthy of respect from contemporary Jews and Christians alike. They caused such an uproar that he was condemned by most mainstream Jewish leaders as an apostate. Even the socialist daily, the *Forverts*, stopped publishing him, and its editor, Abraham Cahan, refused to speak to him any longer. Asch immigrated to Israel in 1953 to escape the furor and died while visiting his daughter in England two years later.

Asch's literary productivity was enormous and much of it has been translated into English. It is easier to find Asch in English translation than any other Yiddish writer with the exceptions of Sholem Aleichem and I. B. Singer. This would only apply to his novels, however; not to his short story collections or plays.

Four of his short stories appear here, including two of his most famous—*Sanctification of the Name (Kidesh ha-Shem)*, (not to be confused with his novel of the same name) and *Kola Street (Koyla Gesl)*. An uncharacteristically light hearted tale, *A Union for Shabbos (A Yunyon af Shabes)*, shows that even orthodox Jews can become solid union men.

Bryna Bercovitch (Ukraine 1894, d. Canada 1956)
Born into poverty, Bercovitch struggled to acquire an education. She became a revolutionary as a teenager and at age 17 volunteered to fight with the Red Army in the Russian Revolution. After the Bolshevik victory, she worked as an actress, a teacher and the director of an orphanage. Due to harsh conditions, she, her husband and children immigrated to Montreal in 1926. She

joined the Communist Party of Canada, but in the late 1930s quit in disgust over the Moscow Trials which charged Lenin's former comrades with treason and led to their execution.

Bercovitch did not begin writing until after 1945, when she became a columnist for Montreal's Yiddish newspaper, *Der Keneder Odler*. For the next nine years until her death she published short stories, literary criticism, political commentary and personal memoirs.

David Bergelson (b. Ukraine 1884, d. Soviet Union 1952)

A prominent Yiddish writer, Bergelson came from wealthy family and received a religious and secular education, studying at the University of Kiev. He began writing in Hebrew and Russian, but turned to Yiddish at Peretz' encouragement. He received plaudits in the Yiddish literary world for his novels *Arum Vokzal (At the Depot)* and *Nokh Aleman (When All is Said and Done)*. His best and most famous novel *Opgang (Descent)*, published in 1920, chronicles the internal decay of a Russian *shtetl* before World War I.

In 1921 Bergelson escaped the turmoil in the Soviet Union and settled in Berlin, where he became a regular correspondent for the Yiddish *Forverts*. He spent six months in the U.S. in 1929 and switched to the communist *Freiheit*. After living two years in Denmark, he returned to the Soviet Union in 1934. There he published a short story collection, *Tvishn Berg (Between Mountains)* and his last novel, *Tsvey Veltn (Two Worlds)*, which suffered from the strictures of Soviet socialist realism. During World War II, he served on the Jewish Anti-Fascist Committee, the voice of Soviet Jewry.

In 1949, during Stalin's anti-Semitic campaign, he was arrested on charges of "Jewish nationalism." He was executed in August 1952 along with many other leading figures of the Soviet Yiddish literary world.

All of the novels cited above are available in English translation.

Lili Berger (b. Poland 1916, d. France 1996)

A literary critic, essayist, novelist, playwright and short story writer, Berger received a traditional religious education and went on to study in a secular Jewish high school in Warsaw. She moved to Paris in 1936 where she taught in Yiddish schools and wrote for the Yiddish press. During World War II, she fought in the French resistance against the Nazi occupation.

After the war she returned to Poland, hoping to help re-establish Jewish life there. She continued to publish in Yiddish and remained until 1968, when the government turned openly anti-Semitic. She then moved back to France. Her works have appeared in Israel, South Africa, France, Mexico and the U.S..

Fishl Bimko (b. Poland, 1890, d. New York 1965)

Although born into a Hasidic family, Bimko became a revolutionary at an early age and spent time in Czarist and German prisons. He immigrated to the U.S. in 1921, where he worked for a few years in garment shops. By this time, he had already written Yiddish stories and plays in Poland.

Bimko continued his literary career in the U.S., primarliy as playwright. His plays were performed at Maurice Schwartz's Yiddish Art Theater in New York City as well as in Poland and Israel. In 1967, the Central Yiddish Culture Organization published a five-volume collection of Bimko's later works, entitled *Ofyn Veg Tsum Lebn (On the Way to Life)*, reflecting his earthy and raw literary style.

Tsvi Eisenman (b. Poland 1920)

One of two living authors whose stories appear in this guide (Elie Wiesel is the other), Eisenman began as a poet, but is better known as a short story writer strongly influenced by the desolation caused by the Holocaust.

He was born in Warsaw to a poor family and received his education in a Yiddish secular school run by a left Zionist organization, an experience that he described as "the deciding factor in my life."

He survived the Holocaust in Soviet Central Asia, returned briefly to Poland, wandered around Central Europe, then immigrated to Palestine, but not before spending two years in a British internment camp in Cyprus. In Israel he was associated with the Young Israel group of Yiddish writers and still lives on a kibbutz. Many of his stories take the form of fables and parables.

Boruch Glazman (b. White Russia 1893, d. New York 1945)
An American Yiddish writer, Glazman immigrated to the U.S. in 1911 from Kiev. He became a house painter by day while attending college at night, graduating from the University of Columbus (Ohio). During World War I, he served in the American army.

His short stories were published in a wide range of Jewish publications in the U.S., Canada, England and Poland. In 1924, he toured Poland and the Soviet Union and remained in Poland for several years before returning to New York in the 1930s. He also wrote in English for American Jewish journals.

Jacob Gordin (b. Ukraine 1853, d. New York, 1909)
Primarily a playwright, Gordin was known as the "king of the Yiddish theater" in New York.

By the time he immigrated to the U.S. in 1891, he already had a checkered career as a Russian writer, a journalist, a farmer and a shipyard worker. In his early years in the U.S. he wrote for both Russian-language and Yiddish newspapers. His friendship with Jewish actors led him to try his hand as a playwright and his career took off after his Yiddish adaptation of Shakespeare's *King Lear* was performed on stage in 1892. Six years later, he had another success with *Mirele Efros*, subtitled the *Yiddish Queen Lear*.

Tremendously popular and influential in Yiddish theater, he adapted or wrote over 70 plays. A quarter of a million mourners lined the streets of the Lower East Side for his funeral procession.

Shira Gorshman (b. Lithuania 1906, d. Israel, 2001)

Born in Lithuania, Gorman and her family were evacuated to Odessa to escape World War I. Self supporting at an early age, she became active in the Zionist movement and immigrated to Palestine in 1924 while still in her teens to work on a kibbutz. By 1930, she moved on to the Soviet Union to work in agricultural cooperatives in the Crimea. She returned to Odessa and then moved to Moscow where she began writing short stories and novels.

In 1998 Gorshman left the Soviet Union for Israel, where she published a memoir in Yiddish about her early experiences.

Chaim Grade (b. Lithuania 1910, d. New York 1982)

One of the last great Yiddish writers to grow to maturity in Eastern Europe, Grade was born into a poor family in Vilna. He studied at a yeshiva established by the Musar movement, which emphasized the necessity of suppressing man's *yetzer hore* (evil impulse). By 1930, he had left this movement to become a secular socialist. He began writing poetry and became an active participant in Vilna's vibrant Yiddish literary scene.

He fled Vilna when the Nazis invaded in 1941, leaving behind his wife and mother, who were murdered. Grade found refuge in the interior of the Soviet Union and returned to Vilna after the war, to discover that the Jewish community there had been totally destroyed.

He immigrated to New York in 1948 and turned to prose in 1950 with the story referenced here. His memoir *Mayn Mame's Shabosim* translated into English as *My Mother's Sabbath Days* is a classic. He also wrote novels about the pre-war world of East European Jews. Some of Grade's work is available in English translation, mainly rendered by his second wife Inna Hecker Grade, who was overly protective of his legacy. With her death in 2010, it is expected that much more will appear.

Sarah Hamer-Jacklyn (b. Poland 1899, d. New York 1975)

Hamer-Jacklyn was born into an observant middle class family that immigrated to Canada when she was still a child. As a young woman, she worked in the millinary trade and then she became an actress and singer on the Yiddish stage. By 29 she began to contribute stories to the Yiddish press in Canada and the U.S. She also wrote a column for the Yiddish daily, *Der Tog*. The subject of her short stories were *shtetl* life and the immigrant experience and revealed how traditional Judaism devalued the lives of Jewish girls.

From her three published short story collections, three stories are referenced here.

Alexander Kapel (b. White Russia 1878, d. New York 1958)

A short story writer and theater critic, Kapel studied at various European universities before beginning his writing career in Warsaw in 1911 with a collection of short stories and sketches. He witnessed the Russian revolution in 1917 and in 1922 immigrated to New York, where he became involved in the Yiddish theater.

Abraham Karpinovitch (b. Vilna 1913, d. Israel 2004)

If Vilna was the last great center of Yiddish culture in Europe, Karpinovitch was one of its last representatives. He belonged to a highly creative family prominent in the worlds of Yiddish theater and literature. His stories and novels recreated life in pre-war Vilna, focusing on outcasts who struggled against harsh conditions to assert their basic humanity.

Karpinovitch spent the war years in the Soviet Union and endured two years of British internment in Cyprus before arriving in Israel in 1950.

Leon Kobrin (b. White Russia 1873, d. New York 1946)

Kobrin was one of the first to write in Yiddish about the American Jewish experience. While in the old country, Kobrin wrote in Russian. Ironically, when he immigrated to the U.S. at age 20, he had not yet mastered Yiddish or discovered Yiddish literature.

As a greenhorn, Kobrin worked in menial jobs in rural Pennsylvania and sweatshops in Philadelphia, Hoboken and New York. He began his literary career as a journalist, developed into a short story writer and finally achieved fame as a playwright. Many of his plays became long running hits in the Yiddish theater. In addition to writing novels, he collaborated with his wife in translating many Russian and French classics into Yiddish. He was also a regular contributor to the Yiddish newspaper *Der Tog* (The Day). His memoir, *Mayne Fuftsik Yor in Amerike (My Fifty Years in America)* was serialized in the *Morgn Freiheit* in the mid-1940s and was published in book form by the YKUF in 1966.

Kobrin's short stories are examples of social realism, infused with a keen understanding of the challenges and generational conflicts faced by Jewish immigrants and profound insight into their often desperate situations. Three such stories are referenced here.

One of his novels, *A Lithuanian Village*, has been translated into English (1920). Its longer Yiddish version was *Fun a Litvish Shtetl biz'n Tenement-Hoyz* (From a Lithuanian Town to a Tenement) (1918).

Rachel Korn (b. Galicia 1898, d. Montreal 1982)

A writer of poetry and prose, Korn grew up on a prosperous farm, an anomaly for East European Jews. She was educated in Vienna, began writing in Polish and only learned Yiddish as an adult. In the 1920s, in the aftermath of pogroms that accompanied the founding of Poland in 1919, she became a Yiddish writer—one of the few Jewish women to appear in literary journals on a regular basis.

When World War II broke out she fled Poland and found refuge in the Soviet Union. Most of her family was murdered during the Holocaust. After the war she returned to Poland and became an official in the Yiddish Writers Union. In 1946, however, she remained in Sweden after attending a writer's conference and obtained visas for other Polish Jewish writers to join her there. Three years later, she immigrated to Canada and settled in Montreal.

Korn published many volumes of poems and stories and her work has been widely translated. In 1974 she was awarded the prestigious

Manger Prize for Yiddish literature from the state of Israel. A website is devoted to her life and work: www.rachelkorn.com

Yankev Kreplak (b. Poland 1885, d. New York 1945)
Fleeing the Russian draft, Kreplak immigrated to the U.S. in 1915. Many of his stories depict the ordeals of Jews in the czarist army. He also wrote children's books in the U.S., including one calling for racial justice, aptly titled *Shvartz un Vays (Black and White)*.

Moyshe Kulbak (b. Lithuania 1896, d. Soviet Union 1940)
Kulbak studied in yeshivas as a youth and started out as a Hebrew teacher and poet. He began writing Yiddish poetry and then turned to novels, stories and plays, some with mystical themes. In 1920 he moved to Berlin and then to Vilna in 1923, where he worked as a Yiddish teacher, much admired by his students and young Yiddish writers.

In 1928 Kulbak returned to the Soviet Union, but his writings never strictly adhered to the party line, His masterpiece, the novel *Zelmenyaner*, concerning the experiences of a Russian Jewish extended family living in the new Soviet Union, was published in 1931. He was arrested during the Stalinist purges in 1937 and was sent to the gulag, where he perished. The Soviet government rehabilitated him posthumously in 1956.

Zelmenyaner, now considered to be among the greatest Jewish novels, has yet to be completely translated into English.

Bertha Lelchuk (b. White Russia 1901, d. California after 1940)
Lelchuk received both a religious and a secular education and lived for a time in Palestine. Before turning to writing, she acted on stage and practiced dentistry. After settling in the U.S. in 1923, she wrote short stories and articles for Yiddish periodicals around the world. Very little is known about her later years. She may have ended up an actress doing bit parts in Hollywood.

Zalman Libin (b. White Russia 1872, d. New York 1955), pen name of Israel Hurwitz

Often paired with Leon Kobrin as pioneers of Yiddish literature in America, Libin also started writing in Russian, came to the U.S. at a young age, worked in sweatshops and achieved success as a writer of Yiddish plays and short stories, based on immigrant Jewish life in America. Unlike Kobrin, however, his first experience of an urban Jewish ghetto was in London, where he lived before coming to America.

His first short story published in the U.S., *"An Arbeters Zifts"* (*"A Workingman's Sigh"*) set the tone for his subsequent stories of social realism, depicting the grueling struggle of the immigrant Jewish workers and their families against poverty and expoitation. He also wrote about the tendency of certain Jewish radicals to repudiate their Jewishness for the sake of universal ideals.

Four of his stories are referenced here.

Helen Londynski (b. Warsaw 1896, d. New York, 1992)

Born into a Hasidic family, Londynski rebelled and studied at a Polish university formed by Jewish socialists. She worked for a Yiddish publishing house in Warsaw, married, and in 1925 moved to Paris. Returning to Warsaw shortly before the outbreak of World War II, she escaped the Nazi invasion and struggled as a refugee in the Middle East, India and southern Africa before arriving in New York in 1942.

She resumed working for Yiddish organizations and wrote poetry and short stories for Yiddish magazines. Two volumes of her poetry have been translated into English. The selection that appears here is taken from her memoirs, published in 1972.

Peretz Markish (b. Ukraine 1895, d. Soviet Union 1952)

Markish grew up in a traditional Jewish household. He served in the Czarist army in World War I and was injured in battle. A novelist, playwright and poet, he left the Soviet Union in 1921 and lived in Warsaw from 1921 to 1926 where he edited Yiddish literary journals and played a major role in the thriving Yiddish cultural scene, primarily as a poet. He also traveled throughout Europe and visited Palestine.

He returned to the Soviet Union in 1926, and he became an outstanding Yiddish literary figure. During World War II, he served on the Jewish Anti-Fascist Committee. He was arrested in 1949 and executed in August 1952, along with other Soviet Yiddish writers and cultural activitist on charges of "Jewish nationalism."

Many of his poems have been translated into Russian and English. His most famous novel, *Dor Oys, Dor Ayn* (Generation After Generation), about the Bolshevik revolution and its impact on Ukrainian Jews, has yet to be translated.

Mendele Moykher Sforim, pen name of Sholem Jacob Abramovitz (b. 1836 Lithuania, d. 1917 Ukraine)

"Moykher Sforim" means bookseller—Mendele's literary persona.

Mendele is the acknowledged "grandfather" of modern Yiddish literature. Before him, Yiddish was considered a vernacular "jargon" whose literature consisted of romances, religious homilies, ethical tracts and folktales fit "only" for women and the uneducated. Mendele and his successors, beginning with Peretz and Sholem Aleichem, elevated its status by introducing more sophisticated characters, plots and themes on par with other national literatures.

He was born into a traditional religious family and attended Yeshiva, but rebelled as a teenager, joining a group of wandering beggars. In short order, he embraced the *Haskalah* or Jewish enlightenment movement, which sought to rid Jews of archaic practices and broaden their minds by introducing them to modern European culture.

Mendele wrote in Hebrew for a decade, producing a three-volume *Natural History*. To reach the Jewish masses, in 1864, he wrote his first story in Yiddish. Thereafter, he wrote in both languages and is considered a pioneer in both modern Yiddish and Hebrew literature. His specialty was the short novel, generally biting satires about the backwardness of Jews in the *shtetl*, the selfishness of their community leaders and the oppressive burden of religious tradition steeped in ignorance.

Among his best known Yiddish works are *Di Takse (The Tax)*, *Fishke der Krumer (Fishke the Lame)*, *Di Klyatsche (The Mare)* and *Benyomin Hashlishi (Benjamin the Third)*. All these and more have been translated into English.

From 1881 he lived mostly in Odessa where he served as principal of a modern Talmud Torah (Jewish high school), while continuing to write. He also collaborated with Chaim Bialik and Yehoshua Ravnitsky in translating the Torah into Yiddish.

Mendele wrote few short stories. Three of his writings are referenced here, two are excerpts from novels (*The Wishing Ring* and *Fishke the Lame*).

Isaac Metzker (b. Galicia 1900, d. New York 1984)
Metzker is one of the few Yiddish writers to describe the experience of Jewish farmers in Eastern Europe, in particular the Austro-Hungarian Empire, where Jews were free to own land. He immigrated to the U.S. in 1924 as a stowaway and became a novelist and short story writer, best known as the editor of "*A Bintel Brief*" the popular advice column for immigrants that appeared for many years in the *Forverts*. He was also a teacher in the Workmen's Circle/*Arbeter Ring* Yiddish *folkshuln* (schools).

His novel, *Oyfn Zeyden's Felder* appears in a 2007 English translation as *Grandfather's Acres*.

Kadya Molodowsky (b. Poland 1894, d. Philadelphia 1975), pen name of Bereza Kartuska
The best known of all Yiddish women writers and the "first lady of Yiddish poetry," Molodowsky had a thorough religious education as a child, an unusul accomplishment for a woman of her generation. She also received a secular Jewish education that

enabled her to become a Yiddish teacher in Warsaw. At a young age, she became active in Yiddish literary circles in Poland and the Ukraine.

In 1935 she immigrated to the U.S., where most of her work was written and published. She wrote children's literature, plays, novels and short stories, but achieved greatest recognition as a poet. Unlike most Yiddish writers who rejected or at least cast a critical eye on traditional Judaism, she tended to romanticize life in the *shtetl*, comparing it favorably with the shallow materialism she found among American Jews. She also stood out in her commitment to Zionism and lived in Israel for three years from 1949 to 1952 before returning to the U.S.. Between 1965 and 1971, she received several literary awards. Her stories and poems for children were published by the Workmen's Circle/*Arbeter Ring* and used in its Yiddish schools. She also edited Yiddish magazines in New York and Tel Aviv.

Thanks to the upsurge in interest in Jewish women writers, her only collection of short stories, *A Shtub Mit Zibn Fentster*, was recently translated and published in 2006 as *A House with Seven Windows*. Five stories from this collection are referenced here.

Joseph Opatoshu (b. Poland 1887, d. New York 1954)

Opatoshu grew up in a village, where he had more contact with non-Jews and the outdoors than the typical Jewish child and attended a Russian elementary school rather than *kheyder* (Jewish religious elementary school). After participating in the 1905 Russian Revolution, which ended in defeat, Opatoshu, like hundreds of thousands of other Jews, immigrated to the U.S., arriving in 1907.

At first, he worked in menial jobs. While attending college at night, he supported himself as a Hebrew teacher. By the 1920s, Opatoshu had become a well-known writer of short stories and historical novels and appeared frequently in the Yiddish press. In his fiction, he often depicted the Jewish underworld, including a famous novella of a family of Jewish horse thieves. He also wrote stories about racism and violence against Blacks in the US, most notably the story *Lintsheray* (Lyching).

Three of his historical novels have been translated into English: *Poilishe Velder (In Polish Woods)*, about Hasidic Jews in 19th century Poland, *A Tog in Regensberg (A Day in Regensberg)* about the Jews in medieval Germany and *Der Letster Oyfshtand (The Last Revolt)* about the Rabbi Akiba and the Bar Kokhba rebellion. His novels were translated into many languages and, like Sholem Asch, he achieved international fame.

Chaver Paver, pen name of Gershon Einbinder (b. Ukraine 1900, d. Los Angeles 1965)

Primarily a children's writer, Chaver Paver taught Jewish refugee children in Rumania before coming to the U.S. in 1923, where he enjoyed a long career as a teacher in left-wing Yiddish secular school.

Chaver Paver also wrote plays and novels for adults about the immigrant experience, including his semi-autobiographical *Gershn Meyer dem Blindens* and *Gershn in Amerika*, parts of which have been translated into English in the collection, *Clinton Street and Other Stories*.

Isaac Leib Peretz (b. Poland 1852, d. Poland 1915)

The intellectual and literary giant of Yiddish literature, Peretz had enormous influence on Jewish thinkers and writers of his generation and beyond as a writer and as an architect of a Yiddish culture. More than any other Yiddish literary figure, he embodied the humanist ideals of Ashkenazic Diaspora Jewry.

Peretz became an attorney and practiced law for 10 years until he was disbarred for political reasons. He wrote in Polish and Hebrew before turning to Yiddish to reach the Jewish masses. Doing research for a Jewish agency, he learned much about Jewish life in the Polish *shtetls*, where the Hasidim predominated. Later, he based many of his short stories on Hasidic folktales. Peretz also was an accomplished poet whose verses were widely recited, put to music and sung by Jews throughout Eastern Europe.

As an intellectual, he was a major voice in the debates and issues that engaged Jews of his era: assimilation, Yiddish, socialism, Zionism and the future of Jews in Europe. He advocated Yiddish cultural nationalism as an alternative to both assimilation and Zionism and supported the Jewish socialist movement while warning against fanaticism. During World War I, in the last year of his life, he devoted his energies to providing relief to homeless and orphaned Jewish children and wrote many poems and songs for them.

His stature was such that young Yiddish writers flocked to his home in Warsaw, seeking his criticism and advice. Many famous Yiddish writers, including Abraham Reisen and David Pinski (see below) are counted among his disciples. Yiddish schools established by secular Jews throughout the world were often named after Peretz and some still bear his name.

Peretz' short stories have been widely translated. (See bibliography) His two best known, *If Not Higher* and *Bontshe the Silent* are referenced here along with fifteen others. *Bontshe the Silent* has been performed on the American stage in both languages.

David Pinski (b. White Russia 1872, d. Israel 1959)

Pinski settled in Warsaw and collaborated on a number of projects with his mentor I.L. Peretz. Before he left for America at age 27, he had already established a reputation as a pioneer of Yiddish proletarian literature. In the U.S., he studied at Columbia University, edited Yiddish newspapers, wrote plays for the Yiddish theater and short stories and novels. One of his finest plays, *Der Oytser (The Treasure)*, a social satire, had the distinction of being produced in Yiddish, English and German.

Pinski's favorite themes were class and generational conflicts and changing attitudes toward marriage and romance. He rejected both religious traditions and assimilation as detrimental to Jewish continuity.

Pinski became involved in the Labor Zionist movement, which deepened his sense of Jewish peoplehood. In 1949 he settled in

Israel, where he continued to promote Yiddish literature and wrote an unfinished series of Biblical dramas.

A collection of his short stories, *Temptations*, was translated into English back in 1919 and reprinted a mere 84 years later in 2003. A number of his plays have also been translated.

Isaac Raboy (b. Ukraine 1882, d. Los Angeles 1944)

Raboy grew up on an estate in Bessarabia, Russia where his father was in charge of the royal mail. As a teenager he rejected traditional Judaism and in 1904 he immigrated to the U.S., where he found work as a hat maker.

Disillusioned with urban life, he enrolled in an agricultural training school in 1908. After graduating, he worked for two years as a farm hand in North Dakota and later wrote about the experience in his novel *Der Yiddisher Kowboy*, which has been translated into English by Nathaniel Shapiro as *The Jewish Cowboy*. He tried his hand at farming in Connecticut, but when that venture failed in 1913, he returned to New York and once again found himself working in the hat trade.

This time, however, he achieved prominence writing for various Yiddish periodicals. He was aligned with the communist *Freiheit* until 1929 when he and other prominent Yiddish writers quit over its defense of the Hebron riots in Palestine, in which Arab mobs massacred 60 Jews. He was among the few that later returned to the communist fold.

In addition to *Der Yiddisher Cowboy*, his novel *Nine Brider (Nine Brothers)* has been translated into English.

Miriam Raskin (b. White Russia 1889, d. New York 1973)

Raskin became a political activist at an early age, joining the Jewish Labor Bund, a revolutionary socialist party that also promoted Yiddish culture. She served one year in a Czarist prison before immigrating to the U.S. in 1920. She wrote short stories for the Yiddish literary journal *Tsukunft* and novels that were serialized in the *Forverts*. Little else is known about her life.

Abraham Reisen (b. Russia 1876, d. New York 1953)

In his time Reisen was one of the most popular Yiddish writers. His poems were often put to music; his short stories published and widely read in the Jewish press.

Born in a Russian *shtetl* to an intellectual family, Reisen gained fame as a young man when he wrote a poem about returning home from military service in the Czar's army. He lived in various Russian and Polish cities working as a writer and as an editor of several Jewish magazines. He sought out Peretz, who read his stories and gave him valuable advice. In 1908, Reisen was a prime mover of a major Yiddish Language Conference in Czernowitz, Rumania, where Yiddish was declared a national language of the Jewish people.

Reisen traveled throughout Europe and America before permanently settling in New York in 1914, after the outbreak of World War I. From 1929 on, his stories regularly appeared in the Yiddish *Forward* (*Forvertz*).

Two of his best stories, *Tuition for the Rebbe* and *Matza for the Rich*, reflect his sympathy for the poor Jews struggling to survive with their dignity intact. Reisen's short stories in English translation appear in many anthologies. There are also two collections, one just published in 2011. (See bibliography.)

Twelve of his stories are referenced here, including the two cited above and the remarkable *Equality of the Sexes* favoring women's equality in personal relationships with men.

Abraham S. Sachs aka **Zaks** (b. Lithuania 1879, d. New Jersey 1931)

A revolutionary in Czarist Russia who immigrated to the U.S. in 1908, Sachs became an editor, journalist, writer and teacher active in the Jewish socialist movement in New York. He wrote economic texts and a history of the *Arbeter Ring*/Workman's Circle, but is best known for his five volume portrayal of the life of Jews in Lithuania, *Khoreve Veltn*, translated into English in a one volume condensed version as *Worlds That Passed*. (See bibliography)

Yente Serdatsky (b. Lithuania 1877, d. New York 1962)

Serdatsky grew up in a literary home and was encouraged by Peretz to become a writer. In 1907, she immigrated to the U.S. and ran soup kitchens for the poor in Chicago and New York. She wrote poetry and short stories for various Yiddish publications, including the *Forverts* and was also known as a playwright. Her selected works in Yiddish were published in 1913, where the referenced story appears. She stopped writing for two decades before resuming her literary career in the late 1940s.

Sholem Aleichem (pen name of Sholem Rabinowitz) (b. Ukraine 1859, d. New York 1916)

"Sholem aleichem" is the traditional Jewish greeting, meaning "Peace be with you," to be answered by "Aleichem sholem."

By far the most popular and most translated Yiddish author, Sholem Aleichem is best known for his humorous, satiric yet affectionate depiction of Jewish life in the *shtetls* of Czarist Russia. His novel, *Tevye the Dairyman*, is the basis for *Fiddler on the Roof.* Another favorite is *Motl the Cantor's Son*, a novel left incomplete at the time of his death, vividly describing the trials and tribulations of an extended Jewish family from its life a Russian *shtetl* through its immigration to America—seen through eyes of a perceptive and playful 10 year old boy.

Sholem Aleichem was fluent in Russian, Hebrew and Yiddish and first wrote in Hebrew before turning to Yiddish to reach the Jewish masses. He grew up in a *shtetl* and as a young man served three years as a government rabbi. He and his family moved to the big city of Kiev, capital of Ukraine, where he lost a fortune in the stock market. After the 1905 revolution and the pogroms that followed, Sholem Aleichem briefly settled in the U.S., but by 1907, he was back in Europe on speaking tours. He was stricken with tuberculosis and spend time convalescing in Switzerland and Italy.

When World War I broke out in 1914, he immigrated to the U.S. for good and died in New York City two years later at only 57. Hundreds of thousands of people lined the streets of the Lower

East Side for his funeral procession and his will was read into the Congressional Record.

Sholom Aleichem's best genre was the short story, but he also wrote novels which read more like short story collections because they were typically serialized in the Yiddish press, as well as plays, essays and a memoir of his youth, *Funem Yarid* (The Great Fair— Scenes from My Childhood).

In 1906, in New York City, he had a famous encounter with Mark Twain where the two literary giants paid tribute to each other as the "American Sholem Aleichem" and the "Jewish Mark Twain."

The only biography of Sholem Aleichem was written by his daughter Marie Waife-Goldberg, entitled *My Father, Sholem Aleichem* (1968). An excellent documentary film *Sholem Aleichem: Laughing in the Darkness*, was released in 2011.

Because of the availability of so many of Sholem Aleichem's short stories in English, his mastery of the genre and the humanism that pervades his writings, 40 of his stories, or about 30% of the total, are referenced in this guide.

Isaac Bashevis Singer (b. Poland 1902, d. New York 1991)

Although Singer was taken to task by Yiddish literary critics for dwelling on the seamy and superstitious side of Jewish life, he nevertheless became the only Yiddish writer to win the Nobel Prize for Literature (1978) and did a great deal to generate interest in Yiddish as a language and a culture. While his novels and short stories have a bleak view of human nature and no use for left-wing ideology of any kind, his output was so vast that there is invariably something in it to appeal to progressive Jews.

Singer grew up in an orthodox Jewish household. His father was a Hasidic *rebbe*, who acted as a judge in personal and community disputes, first in a small town in Poland and then in Warsaw. Overhearing these cases as a boy gave Singer a rich source of material for his later stories, especially the memoir of his youth, *In My Father's Court*.

In 1935 Singer moved to New York where his novels were serialized in the Yiddish daily, the *Forverts*. His breakthrough to the English reader took place in 1950, with the publication of his first novel, *The Family Moskat*, a family saga set in Poland. He next appeared in English in 1953, with the short story *Gimpel the Fool* published in the journal *Partisan Review* and translated by a young Saul Bellow. Thereafter his popularity soared. Some of his novels were written in Yiddish and simultaneously rendered into English. Some of his works only appeared in book form in the translated version. As Singer became more proficient in English, he began to write what some critics claim are two versions of his own stories and novels.

His novels, *Yentl*, about a girl who disguises herself as a Yeshiva *bokher* (student), and *Enemies, A Love Story*, about a Holocaust survivor, were made into Hollywood movies. His life has also been the subject of numerous biographies.

Six of his stories are referenced here, including two children's holiday stories and four personal reminiscences.

Israel Joshua Singer (b. Poland 1893, d. New York 1933)
Isaac Bashevis Singer's older brother was a great Yiddish writer in his own right—primarily as a novelist, although he published a collection of short stories in 1922, while still living in Warsaw. He immigrated to the U.S. in 1933, where he published stories, novels and a memoir about Jewish life in Eastern Europe and America.

His *Di Brider Ashkenazi* (*The Brothers Ashkenazi*) set in the industrial city of Lodz, is a classic of social realism and sibling rivalry. His novel *Yoshe Kalb* was serialized in the *Forverts* and then adapted for the stage, where it achieved great success performed by the Yiddish Art Theater in New York. These and other of his works are widely available in English translation.

He influenced his brother as a writer and also assisted him in getting established first in Warsaw and then in New York. I.B. Singer lovingly dedicated *The Family Moskat* to him. Two of his stories are referenced here—one from his vivid memoir *Of A World That is No More* and the second, a chapter from *The Brothers Ashkenazi*.

Chava Slucka-Kestin (b. Poland 1900, d. Israel 1972)
Born into a poor family in Warsaw, Slucka-Kestin managed nonetheless to study history at the University of Warsaw and graduate from the Jewish Teachers Seminary. She served an internship at YIVO, the Yiddish Research Institute in Vilna, and taught in secular Jewish schools in Poland between the wars. When the Nazis invaded Poland in 1939, she escaped to the Soviet Union.

She returned to Poland after the war, in an effort to rebuild Jewish life. In 1950 she immigrated to Israel, where she became active in the Communist Party.

The story referenced here, about Jewish-Arab intermarriage in Israel, is among the most unusual in this bibliography.

Mordecai Spector (b. 1858 Ukraine, d. 1925 New York)
Born into a Hasidic family, he became secular in his youth. A contemporary and colleague of both Sholem Aleichem and Peretz, he was, in his day, a popular Yiddish novelist who often wrote on humorous themes. His most popular novel *Der Yidisher Muzhik (The Jewish Peasant)* conveyed the Labor Zionist idea that Jews should return to the soil in the land of Israel.

In 1921, he immigrated to the U.S., where he wrote for several Yiddish periodicals. His short stories have been translated into many languages including Hebrew.

Isaiah Spiegel (b. Poland 1906, d. Israel 1990)
Spiegel survived the Holocaust, spending four years in the Lodz ghetto, where he lost his infant daughter before being deported to Auschwitz. He devoted most of his novels and short stories to the tragic fate of Polish Jewry. Some of these stories were written secretly while he was in the Lodz ghetto. After the war, he returned to retrieve them. The referenced story is an excellent example.

Within a few years he immigrated to Israel, where he continued to write in Yiddish, including literary criticism and a novel based on his own life, *Shtaygen Tsum Himl (Stairs to Heaven)*.

I. M. Weissenberg (b. Poland 1881, d. Poland 1938)
Growing up in poverty, Weissenberg became a factory worker in Warsaw and Lodz. His writings reflect his working class origins. Encouraged by Peretz, he wrote short novels and short stories. He depicted the *shtetl* in starkly negative terms—disintegrating due to class divisions and the inroads of revolutionary ideology. Weissenberg typically portrayed tough Jewish characters, although in later years he turned to mystical themes. After Peretz died, he attempted to take over his role as a mentor of young talent.

His socialist realist novella *A Shtetl*, first written in 1906, was translated and published in English in 1973 under the same name and appears in *A Shtetl and Other Yiddish Novellas,* edited by Ruth Wisse (1986).

Elie Wiesel (b. Rumania 1928)
World famous author and winner of the Nobel Peace Prize in 1986, Wiesel was deported to Auschwitz during World War II and nearly perished there. He tried desperately to keep his father alive, but his father contracted dysentery and died a few months before the camp was liberated. After the war, Wiesel was placed in a French orphanage. He remained in Paris, where he attended the Sorbonne, taught Hebrew, became a newspaper correspondent and a supporter of the right-wing Zionist militia *Irgun*.

In 1955, he moved to New York. His many novels, essays and speeches about the Holocaust, written mostly in French, opened the eyes of millions of Jews and non-Jews to the enormity and barbarity of the Nazi genocide against Jews.

The selection referenced here is an excerpt from his first account of his Holocaust experience, *Night*, written in French. It is a condensed version of a much longer account he originally wrote in Yiddish, *Un Di Velt Hot Geshvign (And the World Remained Silent).*

Bibliography (English)

Abramovitsh, S. Y., **The Wishing Ring: A Novel**, Syracuse University Press, 2003

Ansky, S., **The Dybbuk and Other Writings**, Schocken Books, New York, 1992

Asch, Sholem, **Tales of My People**, G.P. Putnam's Sons, New York, 1948

Bark, Sandra, **Beautiful As the Moon, Radiant as the Stars: Jewish Women in Yiddish Stories: An Anthology**, Warner Books, New York, 2003

Dawidowicz, Lucy S., **The Golden Tradition—Jewish Life and Thought in Eastern Europe**, Schocken Books, New York, 1967

Eisenberg, Azriel, **Modern Jewish Life in Literature**, Book 1, United Synagogue Commission on Jewish Education, New York, 1948

Eisenman, Tsvi, **At the Edge of Dreamland**, Ktav Publishing House, Inc., New Jersey, 2008

Fleg, Edmond, **The Jewish Anthology**, Behrman House, New York, 1940

Forman, Frieda; Raicus, Ethel; Swartz, Sarah Silberstein and Wolfe, Margie, **Found Treasures—Stories by Yiddish Women Writers**, Second Story Press, Toronto, 1994

Frieden, Ken, **Classic Yiddish Stories of S.Y. Abramovitsh, Sholem Aleichem and I.L. Peretz**, Syracuse University Press, 2004

Goldberg, Itche, **Yiddish Stories for Young People**, Kinderbuch Publishers, New York, 1966

Goldsmith, Emanuel, **Yiddish Literature in America 1870-2000**, Ktav Publishing House Inc., Jersey City, NJ, 2009

Goodman, Henry, **The New Country—Stories from the Yiddish about life in America**, YKUF Publishers, New York, 1961

Howe, Irving and Greenberg, Eliezer, **Ashes Out of Hope: Fic-

tion by Soviet Yiddish Writers, Schocken, New York, 1977

Howe, Irving and Greenberg, Eliezer, **Selected Stories I. L. Peretz**, Schocken Books, New York, 1974

Howe, Irving and Greenberg, Eliezer, **A Treasury of Yiddish Stories**, Schocken Books, New York, 1953

Howe, Irving and Wisse, Ruth R., **The Best of Sholem Aleichem**, Washington Square Press, New York, 1979

Kantrowitz, Melanie K., and Klepfisz, Irena, **The Tribe of Dina— A Jewish Women's Anthology**, Beacon Press, Boston, 1986

Leftwich, Joseph, **Yisroel: the first Jewish Omnibus**, Beechhurst Press, New York, 1952

Lewis, Jerry D., **Tales of Our People: great stories of the Jew in America**, Bernard Geis Associates, New York, 1969

Liptzin, Sol, **A History of Yiddish Literature**, Jonathan David Publishers, New York, 1985

Liptzin, Sol, **Stories From Peretz**, Hebrew Publishing Company, NY, 1947

Molodowsky, Kadya, **A House With Seven Windows**, Syracuse University Press, Syracuse, NY 2006

Neugroschel, Joachim, **No Star Too Beautiful: Yiddish Stories from 1382 to the Present**, W.W. Norton & Company, New York, 2002

Neugroschel, Joachim, **Shtetl: a creative anthology of Jewish Life in Eastern Europe**, The Overlook Press, Woodstock, New York, 1989

Reisen, Abraham, **The Heart-Stirring Sermon and Other Stories**, The Overlook Press, Woodstock, New York, 1992

Reisen, Abraham, **The Poor Matza**, Windshift Press, Qualicum Beach, British Colombia, 2011

Rosenfeld, Max, **New Yorkish and Other American Yiddish Stories**, Sholem Aleichem Club Press, Philadelphia, Congress of Secular Jewish Organizations, 1995

Rosenfeld, Max, **Pushcarts and Dreamers—Stories of Jewish life in America**, Sholem Aleichem Press, Philadelphia, 1967

Sachs, A. S. **Worlds That Passed**, Jewish Publication Society,

Philadelphia, 1928, 1943

Schwarz, Leo W., **Feast of Leviathan: tales of adventure, faith and love from Jewish literature**, Rinehart, New York 1956

Schwarz, Leo W., **Golden Treasury of Jewish Literature**, Farrar and Reinhart, New York, 1937

Schwarz, Leo, W., **The Jewish Caravan: great stories of twenty-five centuries**, Reinhart and Winston, New York, 1965

Shepard, Richard F. and Levi, Vicki Gold, **Live and Be Well: A Celebration of Yiddish Culture in America**, Rutgers University Press, New Jersey, 2000

Shevrin, Aliza, **Holiday Tales of Sholom Aleichem**, Charles Scribner's Sons, New York, 1979

Shevrin, Aliza, **A Treasury of Sholem Aleichem's Children Stories**, Jason Aronson, Inc., Northvale, New Jersey, 1997

Sholem Aleichem, **Old Country Tales**, G.P. Putnam's Sons, New York, 1966

Sholem Aleichem, **The Adventures of Mottel, the Cantor's Son**, Henry Schuman, New York, 1953

Sholem Aleichem, **The Letters of Menakhem Mendel and Sheyne Sheyndel**, Yale University Press, New Haven, 2002

Sholem Aleichem, **Tevye's Daughters**, Crown Publishers, Inc., NY, 1949

Sholem Aleichem, **Tevye the Dairyman and the Railroad Stories,** Schocken Books, New York, 1987

Sholem Aleichem, **The Old Country**, Crown Publishers, Inc., NY, 1946

Singer, Isaac Bashevis, **In My Father's Court**, New American Library, New York, 1967

Singer, Isaac Bashevis, **Collected Stories: A Friend of Kafka to Passions**, ed. by Ilan Stavans, Library of America, 2004

Singer, Isaac Bashevis, **The Collected Stories of Isaac Bashevis Singer**, Farrar, Straus and Giroux, New York, 1982

Singer, Isaac Bashevis, **Stories for Children**, Farrar, Straus, Giroux, New York, 1992

Singer, Israel Joshua, **Of a World That is No More**, The Vanguard

Press, New York, 1970

Singer, Israel Joshua, **The Brothers Askhenazi**, Alfred A. Knopf, 1965

Tregebov, Rhea, **Arguing with the Storm: Stories by Yiddish Women Writers**, Sumach Press, Toronto, 2007

Waldinger, Albert, **Shining and Shadow: An Anthology of Early Yiddish Stories from the Lower East Side**, Susquehanna University Press, 2006

Weinstein, Miriam, **Prophets & Dreamers: A Selection of Great Yiddish Literature**, Steerforth Press, Vermont, 2002

Wiesel, Elie, **Night**, Hill and Wang, 1960 *(a French translation of a much longer Yiddish version entitled Un Di Velt Hot Geshvign, translated as "And the World Remained Silent")*

Wisse, Ruth R., **The I.L. Peretz Reader**, Schocken Books, New York, 1990

Zuckerman, Marvin; Stillman, Gerald; Herbst, Marion, **Selected Works of Mendele Moykher-Sforim**, Joseph Simon Pangloss Press, New York, 1991

Bibliography (bilingual)

Fridhandler, Louis, **Indexes to the Yiddish Works of Sholem Aleichem and their English translations**, http://yiddish.haifa.ac.il/SholAley/indices.pdf

Katz, Eli, **Yitskhok Leybush Peretz—Selected Stories**, Bilingual Edition, Zhitlovsky Foundation for Jewish Culture, New York, 1991

Two bi-lingual stories from *Pakn Treger*, the journal of the National Yiddish Book Center appear: *Oys Rebe* (No More Rabbi) and *Tamare di Hoykhe* (Tall Tamare). These are available on the NYBC website: www.bikher.org

Bibliography (Yiddish)

All Sholem Aleichem stories come from **Ale Verk Fun Sholem Aleichem, Forverts Oysgabe,** New York, 1942, cited in the text as AV'42, except for *Vayse Kapore (A White Bird)* which is found in **Ale Verk Fun Sholem Aleichem, Folksfond Oysgabe,** New York: Folksfond, 1917-1923

For Peretz stories see **Ale Verk—Y.L. Perets.,** Vilna 1925-29 or **Ale Verk—Y.L. Perets,** New York: Farlag Idish, 1920 for *Dray Matones (Three Gifts), Inem Post-Vogn (In the Mail Coach) and Nile in Gehenem (Ne'ilah in Gehenna), Reb Yoykenen Gabe (Rabbi Yohanan the Warden), Vos Heyst Neshome? (What is Soul?), Tvishn Tsvey Berg (Between Two Mountains), A Klezmer-toyt (The Musician's Death), Der Feter Shakhne un di Mume Yakhne (Uncle Shakhne and Aunt Yakhne) and Der Kunstn-makher (The Magician).* See Katz, Eli, ed., **Yitskhok Lieb Peretz Selected Stories—Bi-lingual Edition (Geklibene Dertseylungen)** for the remaining stories.

For Abraham Reisen stories, see **Ale Verk fun Avrom Reyzin,** New York: Farlag Idish, 1917, unless otherwise noted.

All other Yiddish sources are provided in the text after the summaries of the individual stories.

Some Yiddish short stories are available on the web:

At http://yiddish.haifa.ac.il/stories.html you can find Mendele's *Der Khilef* (The Exchange), Peretz' *Oyb Nisht Nokh Hekher* (If Not Higher), *Bontshe Shvayg* (Bontshe the Silent) and *Sholem Bayis* (Happiness in Marriage), Sholem Aleichem's *Dreyfus in Kasrilevke, Nakhes fun Kinder* (Joys of Parenthood) and *Oysgetreyslt* (A Yom Kippur Scandal) and I.B. Singer's *Tayves* (Passions) among others.

Many (but not all) of the Yiddish originals from Howe and Greenberg's **A Treasury of Yiddish Stories** are available at http://mendele.commons.yale.edu/wp/library/yiddish-texts/onkeles/a-treasury-of-yiddish-stories/ including Asch's *Dos Koyler Gesl* (Kola Street) and *Kidesh Hashem* (Sanctification of the Name), Grade's

Mayn Krig Mit Hersh Raseyner (My Quarrel with Hersh Rasseyner), Peretz' *Bontshe Shvayg* (Bontshe the Silent), *Oyb Nish Nokh Hekher* (If Not Higher),and *Reb Yoykhenen Gabe* (Rabbi Yochanan the Warden), Reisen's *Di Groyse Suke* (The Big Succah) and *Skhar Limud* (Tuition for the Rebbe), Sholem Aleichem's *Dreyfus in Kasrilevke, Oysgetreyslt* (A Yom Kippur Scandal) and Isaiah Spiegel's *Niki* (A Ghetto Dog).

The same website features a few Yiddish stories from **Found Treasures** at http://mendele.commons.yale.edu/wp/library/yiddish-texts/onkeles/found-treasures/ including Sarah Hamer-Jacklyn's *Mayn Mames Kholem* (My Mother's Dream) and Rachel Korn's *Der Letster Veg* (The Road of No Return).

Another page on the Mendele site, http://mendele.commons.yale.edu/wp/library/yiddish-texts/stories-and-novels/ provides more Yiddish stories, including Peretz' *Bontshe Shvayg* (Bontshe the Silent) and *Nile in Gehenem* (Yom Kippur in Hell).

GUIDE TO YIDDISH SHORT STORIES

ABOUT THE AUTHOR

Bennett Muraskin is the adult education director of the Jewish Cultural School and Society in West Orange, NJ. He is the author of *Let Justice Well Up Like Water: Progressive Jews from Hillel to Helen Suzman* (2004), *Humanist Readings in Jewish Folklore* (2001), a co-author of *Celebrating Jewish Holidays: An Introduction for Secular Jewish Families and Their Communities* (2002) along with Lawrence Schofer and Judith Seid. He contributed a chapter on "Jewish Secularism" to *Peace, Justice ad Jews: Reclaiming Our Tradition*, edited by Murray Polner and Stefan Merken (2007). He is a columnist for *Jewish Currents* and *Outlook* (Canada) and a regular contributor to *Humanistic Judaism*. His articles have also appeared in *Israel Horizons*. A much shorter version of this work was published by the Congress of Secular Jewish Organizations (CSJO) in 1997.

Muraskin is employed as a union staff representative for state college professors in New Jersey.

The Association of Jewish Libraries

The Association of Jewish Libraries promotes Jewish literacy through enhancement of libraries and library resources and through leadership for the profession and practitioners of Judaica librarianship. The Association fosters access to information, learning, teaching and research relating to Jews, Judaism, the Jewish experience and Israel.

AJL was established in January 1966 with the merging of the Jewish Librarians Association and the Jewish Library Association.

More information is available at JewishLibraries.org.